PLANNING
AND CREATING
YOUR FIRST GARDEN

Some other titles from How To Books

How to Grow Your Own Food
*A week-by-week guide to wildlife-friendly
fruit and veg gardening*

Meat and Two Veggies
*How to combine meat and vegetarian meals without
having to cook separate dishes*

@ Home with Your Ancestors.com
How to research family history using the internet

The Beginner's Guide to Tracing Your Roots
*An inspirational and encouraging introduction to
discovering your family's past*

howtobooks
Please send for a free copy of the latest catalogue to:
How To Books
Spring Hill House, Spring Hill Road, Begbroke,
Oxford OX5 1RX, United Kingdom
email: info@howtobooks.co.uk
www.howtobooks.co.uk

PLANNING AND CREATING
YOUR FIRST GARDEN

A step-by-step guide to designing your
garden – whatever your experience or knowledge

Paul Power

howtobooks

Published by How To Books Ltd
Spring Hill House, Spring Hill Road,
Begbroke, Oxford OX5 1RX, United Kingdom.
Tel: (01865) 375794. Fax: (01865) 379162
email: info@howtobooks.co.uk
www.howtobooks.co.uk

British Library Cataloguing in Publication Data
A catalogue record for this book is available from the British
Library

ISBN 978 1 84528 187 8

Cover design by Mousemat Design Ltd
Illustrations by Nicki Averill
Produced for How To Books by Deer Park Productions, Tavistock
Typeset by Pantek Arts Ltd, Maidstone, Kent
Printed and bound in Great Britain by Cromwell Press Ltd, Trowbridge, Wiltshire

NOTE: The material contained in this book is set out in good
faith for general guidance and no liability can be accepted
for loss or expense incurred as a result of relying in particular
circumstances on statements made in this book. The laws and
regulations are complex and liable to change, and readers should
check the current positions with the relevant authorities before
making personal arrangements.

CONTENTS

For Dad

PREFACE

I have always loved gardening. As a child I was fortunate to grow up in a house full of love and a garden full of vegetables, shrubs and flowers. Both my parents were keen gardeners and Saturday mornings for as long as I can remember were spent helping my father in our garden. When I left home to start out in life on my own, I lived for a time in rented accommodation until I could afford my first flat, which was located on the second floor of a modern apartment block. Most of communal grounds were devoted to car parking space with some token trees and postage stamp sized lawns, so the closest thing I ever got to real gardening while living there was to feed and water my houseplants.

I had never thought I would miss the countryside as much as I did and I began to spend as much of my free time as I could as far way from the flat as possible.

When I finally had enough of it all, I packed in my job, sold my flat and headed to the Sussex coast where the air is fresh and the soil home to many of the country's finest growers and nurserymen. Few people know for example that many Dutch growers of flowers and vegetables lease and own land in the Sussex area as they believe this is some of the most fertile land in the world.

Faced with the folly of giving up my job, I was forced to re-evaluate my career and reset my life-goals. I started my first gardening business when I was thirteen years of age. It was a simple affair with two clients, the parish priest and an elderly friend of my mother. Accounts were settled on the day and as my reputation grew, so too did my business until my books were full. While my friends spent miserable hours stacking supermarket shelves, manning petrol pumps and cleaning ash trays in pubs, I was out in the fresh air enjoying life to the full and getting paid better than they were. It was a perfect life. The sort of lifestyle you only read about in magazine features. Now at thirty years of age, I was faced with unemployment and a terrible sense of disillusionment. When my mother died from cancer, I promised myself that I wouldn't waste what I had of my own life. So I decided to return to my first business and to the one thing that consistently had given me pleasure and hope in equal measures – gardening.

This book is based upon my own experiences both working with clients on planning and creating their first gardens and our popular gardening workshops – *How to plan and create your first garden*. Each chapter of this book is written with the sole aim of getting you out of your armchair, or out from behind your desk and getting started on creating your first garden. The areas I've covered are those that our clients ask us about the most, including:

◆ How do I come up with a plan for my first garden?
◆ What can I get to grow in a shady, damp area?
◆ How can I transform my garden into something that I really want without it costing the earth?
◆ What sort of tools will I need?
◆ And where should I get them?
◆ What sort of things should I worry about when employing outside help for my project, for example a landscape gardener? Tree surgeon? General Gardener?
◆ What are the pitfalls of doing the job myself and how can they best be avoided?

These are just some of the questions that arise at every *How to plan and create your first garden* workshop. In this book I'm going to show you how to avoid many of the common mistakes made by those new to gardening, but also ways to really turbo-charge your ideas and work your project as a professional gardener would.

HOW TO USE THIS BOOK

Gardening isn't a passive activity. A big part of the planning experience will require you to go out and look, smell, touch and feel what is growing all around you and to take your inspiration from real gardens. Even if you live in a city, there are parks and public gardens where you can visit and see first hand what grows well and where. A damp and shady site should not worry you. Just walk along a country road and see for yourself what grows hidden away from natural sunlight in damp conditions. Touch these flowers, smell them and draw or take photographs of them. The damp, shady site is nothing new to our natural surroundings. Nature has coped brilliantly when faced with seemingly difficult or impossible growing conditions. If you don't believe me, just look at how many weeds grow through pavements and concrete or in the centre of tarmac roads. Given a chance, nature will always find a way.

Did you know, for example, that the reason certain trees shed their leaves in the autumn is because they are fearful of the ground freezing over? Their survival mechanism is such that they shed their water-thirsty leaves in autumn so as to conserve water during the period they expect the ground to be frozen over and water impossible to find. Someone said to me recently that given our current climate their actions seem entirely unnecessary. While this may be the case, trees generally outlive people and I think that given they've discovered the secret of longevity, they probably know what's best for them.

So this book isn't for simply reading – you should use it as a workbook. Complete all the exercises and checklists as you go through each chapter. My advice is based not simply upon my own experiences, but the collective knowledge that has been passed down to us by generations of gardeners. I'm not here to reinvent the wheel or introduce you to some fantastic new gardening techniques, but more to rouse you to action. To nag away at you to pick up a pencil and paper and start planning your garden. And once you've done this to motivate you from paper to soil and to share with you the time – and money-saving tips that have helped us in our business.

Whatever the size of garden that surrounds your home, you should make it your own. A successful garden is one where you, your friends and family can enjoy outdoor living. Gardens are more than simply an extension of our homes. They *are* our homes! Why do so many people fill their lounges with pot plants that swelter, wither and die in their centrally heated houses while concreting over their gardens? Concrete is for living-room floors, gardens are for flowers and nature.

I've created my small courtyard garden to be at times a place where I can find calm and peace away from my busy lifestyle, while at other times my garden is home to regular parties and barbeques. With careful design and planning, I've created a garden where my two dogs, a black Labrador and a boisterous golden retriever, can relax and play without causing damage to the abundance of plants and shrubs that live there.

It's a practical, functional garden where I've managed to meet all of my needs as well as those of my family and pets. Essentially this is what good garden design is all about; making sure that your creation meets all your needs. There's little point in creating a visually impressive ornamental garden if it is to be home to children and a variety of pets. Just like life, gardens are for living people as well as things! A common and understandable mistake is for the novice garden designer to work hard at creating a visually stunning garden while losing sight of their practical needs. Soon their delicate planting arrangements fall prey to children and pets who in no time have decapitated those beautiful flower arrangements and thrown all the shingle onto the lawn.

In my work as a professional gardener, I've seen tempers unnecessarily frayed and otherwise sound relationships threatened because the new garden design has been introduced without really thinking about the needs of those who will be living in it.

Shrubs and plants are just some of the things that your first garden will be home to. More importantly, it will be home to you, your partner, husband, wife, children or pets. Make sure you include their needs in your plans too.

BEWARE THE ULTIMATE LOW-MAINTENANCE SOLUTION

This is where the entire garden is either concreted over or gravelled. Sadly so common are these designs that the result on our environment is that many birds, insects and wildlife have now fled our neighbourhoods and we are all the poorer for it.

By working with nature, we can achieve harmony and balance in our gardens that we can also have in our lives. Stress and competition are now so much a part of our daily lives that more than ever we really do need a calm, natural oasis where we can switch off, recharge our batteries and rediscover the real meaning of life.

I hope that within these pages you find the information you are looking for. I hope that you will be inspired to create somewhere truly special for you to relax, unwind and enjoy yourself.

Gardening is also great fun. In the past few years, I've seen the lives of lots of people of all ages literally transformed by gardening. If at the moment you view gardening as some sort of necessary evil or weekend chore, fine. But don't be surprised when after you get stuck into the planning and creating of your first garden, you become hooked. Lots of successful gardeners that I know started off as reluctant gardeners and have in a very short space of time become expert, knowledgeable and, just as importantly, enthusiastic.

If like many of those who have attended our workshops you are new to gardening, then I hope you won't be put off by any preconceived notions that to garden successfully you must be at it for years. You don't. While undoubtedly with gardening you never stop learning and discovering new things, it's a skill that's within everyone's grasp. Don't get caught up in worrying about making a fool of yourself pronouncing impossible-sounding plant and shrub names. We all struggle with this. Never be embarrassed by any perceived lack of knowledge. I'm forever looking things up and asking other more experienced gardeners for advice.

The most important thing you can do right now is get started. Don't worry about getting it right, that'll come in time. Great gardening is all about being adaptable, flexible and resourceful. Few of us are fortunate enough to have the perfect soil or the ideal climate or the piece of garden that isn't overlooked.

Whatever your site, whatever the problems you can relatively easily plan and create your first garden.

1

WHAT'S INVOLVED IN DESIGNING YOUR GARDEN

GETTING STARTED

Grab yourself a pencil and paper, which I recommend you keep with you at all times when reading this book. When an idea comes into your head or something you really want to remember, jot it down. Ideally you should get yourself a spiral-bound notebook, whatever size you find comfortable. I prefer to use an A5-sized notebook as I find this is just big enough for making rough sketches and just small enough to fit inside my jacket pocket, which means I can take it everywhere with me.

> ### ◆ TIP ◆
>
> Get into the habit of jotting down the names of plants you like, and making sketches of the garden layouts that interest you.

KEEPING A GARDEN JOURNAL

Essentially I use my notebooks as an ongoing Garden Journal. Whenever I come across the name of a plant that I particularly like or is in some way unusual I write the details in my notebook. Wherever possible I make a rough sketch of the plant and underneath this describe its colour or colours. If when I come across any new discovery, I get to speak to someone who owns it, I ask them a few questions as to the plant's likes and dis-likes and how they care for it. I also make a note of what's obvious about the plant. For example, where it's planted – sunny, shady, damp corner, etc. Thus when working on a design or creating a new planting scheme I can refer to my notebook with confidence, knowing that each of the plants and shrubs detailed there hasn't just been taken from a book or catalogue, but has been seen growing in a real garden environment.

The other benefit of keeping a Garden Journal is that as a relatively inexpe-rienced gardener, you can quickly build up your knowledge of gardening by recording what you see and by asking questions of other more experi-enced gardeners.

The sort of information to record in your Garden Journal includes:

◆ The names of plants or shrubs that you find attractive or interesting.
◆ Details of any interesting gardening websites you've come across that might prove useful when planning your garden.
◆ Sketches of garden layouts that you like. For example, when you're out and you find a garden that really interests you, jot down what it is that makes it attractive to you. If possible make a sketch of how it's laid out.

Before going any further, let me give a brief overview of the various stages you'll need to go through to get to the point where you have a final plan for your new garden.

◆ THE STAGES OF PLANNING YOUR FIRST GARDEN ◆

1. Making a rough sketch of your current garden.

2. Deciding what you like and don't like about your present garden.

3. Deciding what sort of features you'd like to include in your new garden.

4. Looking at your existing garden in terms of its potential. How could it be best brought alive and to fulfil all your needs.

5. Making a list of all the features you'd like to include in your new garden.

6. Deciding on what features in your garden you no longer want.

7. There will be some things that you won't be able to get rid of easily or at all. Your new garden design will need to include ways of disguising them.

8. Setting a provisional budget for your project.

9. Working up some rough sketches of what your new garden design will look like.

10. Finalising a working plan for your proposed new garden.

HOW A PROFESSIONAL GARDEN DESIGNER WORKS

Before I take you through the above design process, I want to show first how a professional gardener designs a garden. This is the same method and approach that you should take when designing your first garden. The basic structure designers use for their work is:

1. Find out what their client wants from their new garden.
2. Come up with some ideas as to possible suitable designs, then present to them as 'working drawings.' These drawings are simply rough sketches as to how the new garden might look.
3. Discuss their suggestions with the client. Include the features they liked about the suggested design, lose those features or aspects the client didn't like and come up with a finished garden design.

Although every designer might have a different approach, they'll usually follow roughly the same format as this:

1. Arrange an initial meeting with you at your home to discuss what you'd like from your new garden.
2. Work up a 'Design Brief'. This is basically a checklist of the things you want in your new garden, as well as your preferences in relation to things like colour. The designer will also want to know how much time you're likely to want to spend gardening as this will determine whether they go for a low-maintenance or high-maintenance garden design.

3. Agree a provisional working budget.
4. Carry out a survey of your garden.

All of this will be completed before any design work or ideas are even considered. Once all of the above have been completed, the designer will start on the actual design. Their initial design will be based not only on what you would have told them in terms of your ambitions for your garden, but also from their own observations when meeting you at your home. For example, the décor of your home will indicate what colours you like and also how you like to arrange things. Some people like things neat and tidy while others enjoy a more natural approach. The designer will also get to know more about you and your family. For example, whether or not you have children and/or pets will impact on the design, as whatever the designer comes up with will have to be friendly to your needs.

As you can see, the design process is really nothing more than getting a feel for what you want from your new garden, then offering you a number of potential designs that accommodate all your needs.

Let me explain what each of the terms a professional garden designer uses means.

THE DESIGN BRIEF

The Design Brief is the document that the garden designer will use as a starting point for coming up with a design. It will include as much detailed information as possible about the client they are working for, including: client's colour preferences; the style of garden they would like; information about their current lifestyle; whether or not they want a low- or high-maintenance garden; and as much information as possible about their household – for example, whether or not they have children, pets, relatives staying with them, etc.

In the past when I've designed gardens for clients, I have given them a number of questionnaires to fill in, which gather the information outlined above. This information gives me a greater chance of coming up with a garden design that meets all their needs.

In the next chapter you'll be completing similar questionnaires, which will help you when working out a new design for your garden.

THE GARDEN SURVEY

Once the designer has completed the Design Brief, they will turn their attention to your garden. The Garden Survey is simply a matter of recording as much information as possible about your garden.

Later, I'll show you how you can carry out a simple but effective survey of your own garden. The main benefit of carrying out a survey of your garden is that you'll gain a greater appreciation of its potential as well as possible limitations and any problems that will need to be addressed.

A Garden Survey will include:

◆ Measuring the overall size of your garden.
◆ Determining the type of soil your garden has.
◆ Determining your garden's aspects. For example, you may have a north-facing front garden and a south-facing rear garden.
◆ Recording an inventory of plants, shrubs and trees that already exist in your garden.
◆ Flagging up potential problem areas. For example, any damp, dark areas or areas where the soil is poor and requires improvement.
◆ Environmental features local to your garden. For example, you may have a manhole cover somewhere in your front lawn or a telegraph pole in your side garden area.
◆ Recording existing focal points that could be used when planning the new garden design. For example, you may already have a beautiful tree in your front garden that you would like to become the focus of attention in the new garden.
◆ The positions of things like outside taps, garden buildings, gates, access points, etc.
◆ Any other information that will help the garden designer come up with their final design.

BUDGET

Before putting pen to paper, the garden designer will need to know how much money you intend to spend on creating your new garden. There's little point in a designer coming up with an elaborate new garden design if you're not going to be able to create it through lack of funds. So prior to working on the design they will want to know how much money you have available.

In the past when I've designed gardens for clients, some of them have been particularly vague when I mention budgets. 'Oh just come up with some-thing and we'll see if we like it . . .', they say. I've never designed on that basis and I don't recommend you do either. There's little point in spending time creating a wonderful new design for your garden if ultimately it will never be created owing to a lack of money.

There's nothing wrong at all with having little or no money to create your new garden. That's fine. You can work within that and look at ways of cre-ating your design around the budget constraints. What you should never do is start off with the idea that you're going to create something but with no idea of how much money you have available to do it.

THE GARDEN DESIGN

The final thing the garden designer will come up with is the design itself. As you can see, far from simply sitting down and coming up with a design, there is a process to be followed, which includes gathering information and analysing what's already in your garden.

The advantage of designing your own garden is that undoubtedly you are the best-placed person to do this. I've written this book as a sort of step-by-step guide for you to design and create your own garden. I hope that by introducing you to the way a professional designer works you can see the stages you're going to have to go through before you even get to start on your design. The advantage of this is that you're never going to be faced with a blank page on which to create your design. Instead, working with me you're going to build up a picture of what it is you want from your garden and what you can hope to achieve given your garden's soil and climatic conditions, while keeping a firm eye on how much you have available to spend.

SOME BASIC EQUIPMENT TO GET STARTED

All you'll need to get started are:

◆ **Notebook** – Preferably a hardbacked spiral-bound notebook either A5 or A4 size. Hardback is useful as you can take notes and sketch while standing up. Spiral-bound makes it easier to flick through pages with less possibility of the pages and binding coming apart.
◆ **HB pencil** – In damp conditions it's always easier to write with a pencil as opposed to a biro.
◆ **Builder's measuring tape** – Preferably one that's about 30 metres long and winds up into a case after you've finished measuring. You'll need the tape when you come to surveying your garden.
◆ **Soil testing kit** – Available in most good garden centres or from online garden retailers.
◆ **Digital Camera** – Not as essential as the other things, but if you have a camera it can be very useful in photographing your garden as it is now so you can study it while working elsewhere. A camera is great to record other garden designs, shrubs and materials that interest you, but remember there's no real substitute for sketching.

THE SEVEN SINS OF AMATEUR GARDEN DESIGN

Before going any further, I want to introduce the seven sins of amateur garden design. These mistakes are easily made and you may actually find a number of them familiar to you when reading through them. I'm of the opinion that if you become aware of them at this early stage in your project, they'll be much easier to avoid.

1. The garden that doesn't flow.
2. The Grave Syndrome.
3. The garden that lacks seasonal interest.
4. The low-impact, high-maintenance garden.

5. Themed gardens.
6. Working with no clear design plan.
7. Failing to set a budget.

1. The garden that doesn't flow

I've put this as my number one deadly sin because in my experience it is the most common mistake and also the one that causes the most ongoing problems. The main problem with the garden that doesn't flow is that rather than having one rectifiable mistake, the garden is made up of a series of major blunders, which can include any of the following:

◆ Paths that are too narrow for walking through where you risk the danger of being attacked by shrubbery or a head injury if someone's left a window open.

◆ Gates that have to be forced open and when open are too narrow to push a lawn mower or wheelbarrow through.

◆ Lawns that include areas which are too small for a lawn mower to go over and consequently you need either to go down on bended knees with clipping shears or, worse, a pair of scissors. I kid you not.

◆ Hedges that are impossible to trim because directly in front of them are unmovable objects or features, for example – large flower borders, greenhouses, garden sheds, etc.

◆ Shrubs and trees planted too close to buildings so that they're constantly getting in the way and having to be cut back.

◆ Gardens in which every time you attempt to do something your efforts are hampered by something else getting in your way.

Make no mistake about it – these gardens exist in great numbers, and the determination of their creators to maintain these non-flow, no-go environments contrary to all advice is frightening.

I've worked in gardens where I'd have to employ two gardeners to work on a job that should've taken one person. The reason a second person was needed was to help lift the gardening machinery over fences and up impossibly steep pathways and even on occasions over rear fences because the pathways have either been too narrow or otherwise obstructed.

I've worked in some gardens where the simple and otherwise usually enjoyable act of cutting a hedge has turned into a major feat requiring the dexterity of a circus trapeze artist to hang over greenhouses, sheds, garages and abandoned caravans. On one memorable occasion I had to cut a rear boundary hedge that was over four metres tall but with a large carp  pond that the homeowner had decided to place directly in front of it. We had to build a temporary frame over the pond, upon which we then laid sheets of plywood so that we had a platform to put our ladders on. While this is an extreme example, the owners of the garden said to me that when they'd created the fish pond they'd never really given much thought to how in the future they'd cut the hedge.

Ultimately, what all 'non-flow gardens' have in common is the capacity to make the otherwise sedate pastime of gardening a complete nightmare.

We'll look later at what's involved in avoiding this first sin, but for now it's important to recognise the problems caused when a garden is created without any thought to how it flows, how one can navigate round it or easily undertake common and regular gardening tasks.

2. The Grave Syndrome

Or what's commonly mistakenly referred to as 'the low-maintenance garden'. In other words, one where you remove any hint whatsoever of anything living and replace it with either a mixture of ornate chippings, flagstones and concrete or simply chippings. On top of which is generally placed a plastic birdbath, with a number of colourful plastic butterflies stuck to the end wall. Sadly, I have witnessed the destruction of otherwise beautiful gardens in favour of these low-maintenance graves.

Indeed, so great is the problem these gardens cause that bird populations and wildlife in certain areas are becoming extinct. Ironically, there is nothing low maintenance about these gardens. In no time at all the shingle starts to discolour, fills up with leaves blown from neighbouring gardens or other green debris, which starts its own microclimate as weeds start to grow uninvited at often alarming speed, and the whole area becomes an overgrown mess. All that remains is the now-discoloured resin birdbath that has failed to deliver on its promise of bringing birds to the otherwise barren garden.

3. The garden that lacks seasonal interest

I can never understand those people whose borders are full of soil, which they meticulously weed throughout the year waiting for those summer months when they dot them full of uninspiring bedding plants. The meticulous monotony of winter time weeding is then replaced with a spring and summer regime of endless dead-heading, nocturnal watering and wishing the neighbour's cat would fall under some passing traffic.

The magic of gardening is in working with the seasons and creating a garden that interests and inspires all year round. There is no need for you to stare at empty soil borders through those long wintry months when you could be enjoying watching the seasons come and go through different plants. Surely one of the most beautiful sights is to see trees change to their autumnal colours and then burst into new growth in spring? This is an effect that's not only far easier to create than having to replant endless rows of bedding plants, but also costs considerably less.

So when we come to the actual designing stage for your garden I want you to create a garden with all-year round interest. One where you wake up on a dreary winter's morning there'll be something out there to cheer you up, inspire or interest you. Whatever it is – even if it annoys you – it's surely better than looking at empty soil borders waiting for the next round of winter weeding.

4. The low-impact, high-maintenance garden

The opposite extreme is when gardens are created that are fully planted all year round with shrubs and plants that require continual attention. While there's nothing wrong with this approach, provided of course you've lots of time for gardening, it can all be wasted if the overall garden design lacks impact. For example, a garden with lawns, green hedges, green shrubs and evergreen trees can be quite monotonous. While nowhere near as bad as the Grave Syndrome garden, the low-impact garden creates a feeling of boredom and lacks focus and interest. The problem then is that as the garden starts to look the same all over the owners stop maintaining it, as all they're really doing is cutting things back as opposed to bringing things on. Fairly soon the whole thing becomes an overgrown mess through lack of interest, energy and enthusiasm.

The importance of creating balance in your garden will become apparent as you move through the book. But for now all you need to be aware of is that too much of anything in your garden can quickly lead to monotony, which then becomes hard work.

5. Themed gardens

Rarely can I say I've seen a themed garden that worked well. The problem is that for, say, a Mediterranean-style garden to work without looking contrived, everything surrounding the garden must be Mediterranean too. How many times have you driven by a red-bricked, box terraced house and seen attempts at creating a Mediterranean garden? They stick out like a blister on the street because they're not in keeping with their surroundings. When it comes to designing your garden, don't ignore your home itself and of course your neighbourhood. While undoubtedly you can create your own perfect oasis amid inner-city decay, the secret is to create it so that when you're outside on the street your cannot see in and when you're inside your garden you are unaware of what's going on outside.

Later in the book, when we come to looking at choosing a particular style of garden, I'll show you what's involved in creating an authentic Mediterranean garden, cottage garden and formal garden. You'll then be able to decide for yourself whether or not a particular style is suitable for you. At this early stage, don't be too hung up on one particular style. Far better for you to keep an open mind and be open to a number of different styles than try to shoe-horn a particular design into your garden.

6. Working with no clear design plan

Far too many people seem to wake up one morning and decide to give their garden a complete makeover. Rather than stop and spend some time planning their project, they rush out shovel in hand without any clear plan of what it is they're trying to achieve and end up getting frustrated and despondent.

For a garden design to be successful it needs to work on a number of levels:

◆ It needs to be able to accommodate all of your lifestyle requirements. For example, if you have children or pets, your garden will need to be created in such a way that it offers a safe area for them to play in.
◆ If you like outdoor entertaining, your garden needs to be able to host your barbecues and parties with ample space for your guests to relax and enjoy themselves.
◆ If you love the idea of growing your own fruit and vegetables you'll need to have a suitable area in your garden in which to do this.
◆ If at the moment your garden is a long, narrow, boring plot, you're going to have to come up with a design that makes it more interesting, intriguing and one in which the shape isn't immediately obvious.

If you start off with a clear plan of how you can address your needs and those of your family then you really are halfway towards creating the garden of your dreams. Working with no plan or without any clearly defined objectives means that your garden is going to simply happen as opposed to be created. In my experience I've never seen a great garden happen. Great gardens are planned right down to the last shrub.

7. Failing to set a budget

Earlier, I touched on the importance of creating a financial budget. Nothing is worse than seeing an unfinished garden project. How many times – perhaps this even applies to you – have you seen either your neighbours', friends' or relatives' gardens a virtual building site complete with blue tarpaulin sheets, stacks of mouldy paving slabs, rusty wheelbarrows and the like? Sadly it's a common sight and one which with a little bit of planning can be avoided.

There are two budgets you have to consider:

1. Financial budget.
2. Time available to complete the project.

The financial budget, as I said earlier, is something you must get right. Obviously nothing will bring your project to a grinding halt quicker than running out of money. But what about running out of time? Over the years I've seen so many promising gardens come to a halt because their creators simply ran of out time. The project then got suspended and the unfinished garden got left for another season, which got left again because of the foreign holiday, camping trip or whatever.

My experience is that whatever garden you're going to design and create, you should set yourself a goal of finishing your project within one season. If your garden is so large that this is going to be impossible, consider breaking it up into seasonal objectives. For example, tackle the front this year and leave the back until next year, or tackle it section by section.

Timing is important when you're creating your garden. If you're reading this book in late summer, then remember that fairly soon Autumn will be here and those long, bright evenings will no longer be with us, thereby reducing the daylight available to work on your garden. Were you to start in early spring you'd have the advantage of looking forward to longer days and hopefully better weather.

Avoid the sins

While there's nothing wrong with making mistakes – after all, gardening is essentially trial and error – what's unforgivable is wasting time and money on a project that's ultimately going to frustrate you. While the seven deadly sins in no way cover all the potential trips and falls that await you, they do nevertheless make you aware of the more obvious ones.

◆ CHECKLIST ◆

◆ To get started on your project you'll need a notebook, pencil, builder's measuring tape and if possible a digital camera.

◆ Designing your garden is achieved by working through a number of stages.

◆ You can reach your goal by following the same system that a professional garden designer uses.

◆ Read through again and become familiar with the seven sins of amateur garden design. They are easily made and, once done, difficult to undo.

◆ Start thinking now about budgets, both in terms of how much money you have for your project and how much time you have available. The way to save time and money on your project is to set clear budgets from the very beginning.

◆ Great gardens don't happen, they're planned. If you haven't got the time to plan all of your garden, then break your garden up into smaller sections and work your way through these.

2

THE FIRST STEPS IN THE DESIGN PROCESS

HOW YOUR LIFESTYLE IMPACTS ON YOUR GARDEN DESIGN

As I explained in Chapter 1, professional garden designers work on the basis of finding out as much as they can about their clients in terms of their needs, likes and dislikes and also how much money they have available to create their new garden.

With this project, you are your client. So your first priority is to work on identifying your own needs, likes, dislikes and those of any family and/or pets who are going to be sharing your new garden.

There are three main 'needs' areas you should concentrate on:

1. Your practical needs.
2. The needs of those who live with you.
3. Your inspirational needs.

NEEDS QUESTIONNAIRES

Time to complete your Needs Questionnaires. Questions asked here are the same questions a professional garden designer would ask you when working on his Design Brief.

◆ **TIP** ◆

> Completing these questionnaires is probably the most important part of the design process, as the information you record here will form the foundation on which you can build your new garden design.

Read through the questions below and pencil in your thoughts, then a few days later, re-read them and see if you're still happy with what you've written. Where possible, you should also discuss the answers with the rest of your family. It's important to get everyone's opinions at this early stage so you can avoid potential conflict or misunderstanding when the project is underway.

YOUR PRACTICAL NEEDS CHECKLIST

◆ How many garden areas do you have in your home? For example, some people might only have a rear garden, while others will have a front, rear and possibly side gardens.

◆ Are you planning to redesign all the garden areas or are you just going to work on one area? If your garden is particularly large you may want to break the project down into more manageable areas. For example, front garden this year, rear garden next year.

◆ Do you intend to grow your own vegetables, fruit and herbs? If so, then what size of area are you going to devote to produce production and where are you going to locate it in the overall garden plan?

◆ How much time will you have available for gardening in your new garden? Be realistic here. If you're time poor, then a high-maintenance garden plan is not going to be for you unless you're planning to hire a gardener to help you. If you've lots of time, or you really love gardening, then obviously you want a high-maintenance garden where you can indulge yourself in your favourite pastime.

◆ If you have a car or cars in your household, is there sufficient space for car parking or will you need to redesign your garden to make more space available?

◆ Is there any area of your garden that is very steep and where you might have to consider having steps built?

- Have you got sufficiently wide footpaths to navigate around your home and garden?
- Do you intend to dry your clothes outside? If so, have you got a suitable area for drying them on a line or to erect a rotary dryer? How do you get to the rotary dryer? In the event of a sudden downpour, do you have to make your way over wet grass to your dryer or clothes line or do you have a relatively dry, safe pathway?
- In its present state, is your garden safe and secure for every member of your household, including children and pets? For example, have you gates in all the right places, and are they secure? Or have you an existing large pond that will cause a potential hazard to young children? In 2004, fourteen children drowned in garden ponds.
- Have you sufficient means to water your new garden? Don't just think outdoor taps here, but try to include some water butts and perhaps a system for using 'grey' water to water your garden. Grey water is the water you use to bathe in and wash dishes in.
- Overall security. Is your garden vulnerable to unwanted visitors? For example, would the inclusion of a high prickly hedge in your new design prove a deterrent to anyone wanting to climb over your walls or fences? Or do your existing boundaries need to be renewed or replaced?
- Environmental hazard. Is there something in the local environment that encroaches on the enjoyment of your garden that you will need to address in the new design. For example, clients of mine lived behind a school play yard. For their new garden design they wanted me to come up with ways of reducing the noise and stopping the children from climbing through the fence.
- Budget. Time and money should always be a practical concern for your new project. How much time and money have you available to devote to your new garden? Rough figures and estimates will do. The most important thing is to start thinking about this important area.

As you can see, your practical needs are the sort of mundane things that in my experience often get overlooked by those new to garden design. It's important to make sure your new garden is both practical and inspirational.

THE NEEDS OF THOSE WHO LIVE WITH YOU

If you've completed your needs checklist you'll see there are a number of questions relating to the rest of your household. If you don't live alone, then it's time to consider the needs of those who live in your household.

◆ If your children are of a certain age then it's essential that you create a safe area for them to play in where they won't run the risk of damaging any delicate planting that you might have in mind. Most of us spend a great deal of time in our kitchens so if you are considering where to situate your children's play area, make sure it's a place were you can easily see at a glance what they're up to and make sure their safe.

◆ Pets. I have two dogs and a small courtyard. My courtyard is designed to be dog-friendly. By erecting trellising around the border, I've managed to keep the dogs away from damaging the shrubbery and plants. This way, I can enjoy my garden and they can still relax and play there without causing too much destruction.

◆ Elderly members of your household. If you have elderly persons or people with limited mobility living with you then you'll need to consider their needs. For example, if you have some steep steps, could you replace these steps with a gently sloping pathway?

YOUR INSPIRATIONAL NEEDS

Inspirational needs covers your creative side, personal tastes in terms of textures, colours, etc., and what really moves you when it comes to your garden.

◆ Write a list of your favourite colours and ones that you'd like to see more of in your garden. Don't worry at this stage about trying to come up with plants to match your colours, you can do this later.

◆ Would you like your garden to be in a formal style, where it appears very planned with a not a blade of grass out of place. Or an informal style, with plants spilling onto plants, a variety of shrubbery, trees and lots of dense planting arrangements?

◆ Is there a particular material that inspires you? For example, some people might have a preference for cobbled paths and natural stone patios, while others prefer to have paving slabs. Similarly some people tend towards stone patios for seating areas, while others favour raised decking areas. It's all a matter of personal choice, and at this stage don't look for right or wrong answers. Just note down your preferences.

◆ Look to your senses when thinking about what inspires you. Is there a particular scented plant that brings back great memories of something special in your life? Or maybe a certain smell has the opposite effect. One of my clients had a real disliking for the smell of lavender as it reminded her of a relative who had once been cruel to her.

The above checklists are by no means definitive, but they give you an idea of the sort of things you need to be thinking about and making some early decisions on. If you're planning to live out your days in the home you live in now, don't forget to think about your future needs. For example, fences require far more maintenance than walls. So if you have fencing you might like to consider replacing it with a brick wall, or of course better still creating a living boundary and planting a hedge. I'll show you what's involved with planting hedges later in the book, but for now just concentrate on planning.

SEEING YOUR GARDEN AS AN EXTENSION OF YOUR HOME

Over the course of running my garden design workshops, I always try to get everyone to move away from the image of a garden being simply an area where you occasionally sit, frequently weed and water, and get annoyed when the lawn mower doesn't live up to what the salesperson said it would do. A well-planned garden will be an extension of your home, albeit outside.

Therefore when planning your new outdoor space you need first to look inside your own home. You might find this odd, but every garden designer that I know, including myself, will always want to have a look at how your home is. What we're looking for here isn't just what colours or textures you like, but more importantly what type of lifestyle you lead. For example, do you live alone or with a house full of children and pets? When the new garden is completed, how much time will you realistically have to maintain it? If when I visit, I see you have piles of ironing, undone dishwashing and general untidiness, I know that despite what you might say, your new garden is going to have to be low maintenance and capable of self-sufficiency.

EXERCISE

Time to get out in your garden

Once you've completed your checklists, you're ready to have a closer look at what's really going on in your garden. Even if it's wet and damp out there or blowing a storm, I suggest you leave wherever you are right now and venture out into your garden. Take with you your trusty notebook and pencil. The advantage of doing this right now, unless of course it's pitch dark outside, is that you get to see your garden as it is right now. Not as you remember it, or as you visualise it might be, but as it really is.

THE SENSORY WALK – WHAT YOU SEE, HEAR, SMELL AND FEEL

The objective here is simply to step outside whatever door you would normally use to enter your garden and stand there for a moment or two. Breathe in and take some air. Close your eyes for a few moments and try for a while to rely on senses other than what you see. What can you hear? Can you hear lots of passing traffic or neighbourhood noise? Or is your garden already tranquil and peaceful? If it is, is it always like this? Or is it because of the time of the day you're undertaking this exercise? What can you smell? What can you feel? The warmth of the sun? The wind?

When you open your eyes write down:

- The sounds you heard.
- How you feel about them. Do they make you feel stressed and angry or is your garden calm and peaceful?
- Any noticeable natural smells? Can you smell any of your existing shrubs, plants or flowers? Or those of any neighbours?
- Did anything particularly move you? Was it something that might seem trivial, like you never really noticed how windy just outside your back door can be?
- What about light? Even with your eyes shut, you'll be able to determine the impact of light on your face. It's a little like sunbathing when you lie in the sun and even with your eyes closed you can tell by the change in darkness if the sun has gone behind some clouds. If it's a sunny day

when you do this exercise are you standing in the sun or shade? If it's the shade is it shady because something is blocking the light from getting in or is it a case of a north-facing area, time of the day, etc?

Record your findings in your notebook

Write it all down. Remember you're the garden designer trying to find out as much information as you can about your garden. Making notes will help you focus on what you've seen and highlight areas that you wouldn't have otherwise considered. It doesn't matter if it's barely legible because your hands are frozen! The important thing is to make as many notes as you can about the impact that simply standing outside your house has on you. It doesn't matter at this stage if this is all you have time to do. Just get out there and enjoy getting started.

The next stage

Once you've completed the initial stage, I want you to venture out into your garden again. It doesn't matter if you do this at the same time as the previous stage. The important thing is that you get out there and do this as soon as you possibly can. Don't put it off until you finish reading this book. Get working on this right away as the information you're gathering will form the foundation from which you're going to create your garden plan. If like me you only have a tiny courtyard garden then simply stand or sit on your doorstep. If you're reading this book somewhere where you cannot undertake the exercise then close your eyes and try to visualise yourself walking through your garden recording the necessary information as you continue along your virtual walk.

What you're looking to do here is to make three distinctive lists, which will include:

1. What you really dislike about your current garden.
2. What things you like or at least are happy enough with to keep them in your new garden.
3. What things you don't like, but you can't get rid of them.

WHAT DON'T YOU LIKE ABOUT YOUR PRESENT GARDEN?

Be brutal here. Include everything you dislike about your garden from the colour of the fence or boundary wall to the shrubs that you really want to see the back of. Remember at this stage you're only working up a list. You're not actually confirming the death or demise of anything. Be on the lookout for those seven deadly sins. For example, how does your present garden flow? Do you have to perform a trapeze act everytime you want to cut the lawn. Or perhaps you feel that your garden is too overlooked. Perhaps your garden is one of those that has a low-level boundary fence, which means that whenever you venture out you are forced to make polite conversation. Whatever irritates you, write it down. If you find there's nothing out there to annoy you then have a look through my pet-hates list, which I've compiled from speaking to my customers as well as including my own thoughts.

The gardener's pet-hates list
◆ Shrubs, trees or other foliage that block light from their gardens.
◆ Untidy adjacent gardens.
◆ Pathways that are too small to navigate along.
◆ Lawns with areas that are either moss-ridden, bare-patched or otherwise unsightly.
◆ Ugly or intrusive boundary fences, walls and hedges.
◆ Traffic noise.
◆ Neighbour noise.
◆ Neighbourhood smells, including traffic odours or other odours caused by polluted rivers, factories, civic amenity tips and so on.

Most irritants will be sensory-based
As you can see from the list the main irritants are what I call *sensory*-based, which means whatever it is that annoys you you'll be able to see, hear, smell or feel.

For example, noise and either lack of light or too much light (street lighting intruding into the home at night) always feature top on the list of gardeners' pet hates. Unpleasant odours also feature strongly and in my experience act as one of the common motivators for homeowners wanting to redesign their gardens. Unwanted odours can be anything from fumes

from passing road traffic to those generated by local industry or even local takeaway restaurants and the like. Where this is the case, usually all the houses in the neighbourhood will suffer from the same problem, so it's worth looking at your neighbours' gardens to see what, if anything, they have done to ease the problem.

When you have generated your list of dislikes you will start to see some of the problems that your new garden design should be addressing, but that perhaps previously you hadn't thought of. My idea of planning the perfect garden is to forget the gazebos, water features and so on until after such time as you've addressed the real problems. Once you've addressed these the rest is easy. Anyone can come up with a design that incorporates a plastic pond with a waterfall and dot around a few palm trees to give a supposed Mediterranean garden. But it takes a bit more skill to turn an otherwise unfriendly, perhaps even inhospitable, garden into your own oasis. As this book is about achieving the impossible, let's start working on removing those things that cause you the most stress. Then we can concentrate on the things that will bring you the most joy! If you get this right then you really will create your perfect garden.

Some years ago together with my partner we purchased what we thought was an idyllic bungalow on a large corner plot. The garden, although in a fairly overgrown state, oozed potential. I couldn't wait until we moved into the house so that I could get to work on the garden. As it was autumn the first thing I did was make preparations to include a herb and vegetable garden as close to the kitchen door as I could. When that was underway I worked on the lawn area, improving what was a weedy, miserable moss-covered pitch to a brilliant green carpet of lush grass. During my spare time I worked away at rejuvenating the neglected plants, shrubs and trees.

What I didn't do was take any notice of the perimeter larch lap fence, which would ultimately be my undoing. Because as spring came and went and my veggies, lawn and shrubs began to flourish, the fence fell into further disrepair. Finally one night I was awoken during a particularly bad storm to the sounds of crashing and glass smashing. I pulled on whatever clothes were nearest my bed, rushed out into the garden and got flattened by a flying fence panel. Lying on my back with the wind and rain howling around me, I realised all too late my error – it was to ignore what I detested the most, the perimeter fence. Even though at the time my gardening business included a fencing company, I detested anything to do with fence erection or repairs. Therefore the fence was the one job that had been put on that to-do list that you know you'll never get around to doing.

The following morning I surveyed the damage. Almost everything I had worked on over the course of the previous autumn and winter had been damaged. Some of it, particularly what was inside the greenhouse, had been destroyed completely. It took weeks to remove the shards of glass from the surrounding lawns and borders.

Demotivated and kicking myself for being so stupid, I continued rebuilding the garden. What should have been completed in a year took over two, during which time the enjoyment of gardening became more of a chore, as anyone who has ever had to do a job twice will tell you. The first time round everything is fun, novel and you're filled with a sense of excitement, but when forced to rebuild, re-erect, replant and redo a garden that you've only just finished it's difficult to make it happy work.

EXERCISE – CREATE YOUR LISTS OF LIKES AND DISLIKES

The important thing is to get to grips with your dislikes as early in the process as you can. Don't overlook things that are going to spoil you enjoying your garden. Create your list of dislikes with care and you'll have great fun either getting rid of them when the time comes to create your new garden.

WHAT DO YOU REALLY LIKE ABOUT YOUR PRESENT GARDEN?

The reason it's important to jot down the things you like about your garden is that these then become the positives that we will focus on when it comes to working out your design. I've also seen instances where in the excitement of a garden makeover the good as well as the bad gets destroyed.

On one project we worked on I witnessed the husband eagerly cutting down an apple tree, which his wife had wanted to keep. When I urged caution, he simply said: 'Doesn't matter, if she wants another one we can plant another one.' Which is true, of course. The only problem was I estimated the apple tree to be well over thirty years old. So while you can plant another one you've a thirty year or so wait until it comes anywhere near the size and shape of the original one.

Gardening mistakes are easily made and difficult to rectify, which is why working to a clear plan is the only way to avoid losing something you really want to keep. Include as much as you can in your list and try to describe why it is that you like one thing over another. A little note is all you need. For example: 'I like the tree in the corner border. Be ideal for providing shade on a hot summer day.'

The list will focus your preferences, but equally it will ensure that you don't make the mistake of overplanting or creating too much of the same thing just because you like it, which can be an easy mistake to make. Some people I know just love dwarf conifer trees, which they plant everywhere, making their garden look a little bit like a Christmas tree farm. Or others love a certain type of bedding plant, which they then dot around the garden in great circles and row after row, making the garden look contrived, gaudy and boring.

What you're looking for in your ultimate design is a balance, as opposed to an overreliance on one feature, plant, shrub or colour.

WHAT YOU DON'T LIKE, BUT CANNOT GET RID OF

When you've finished with your likes and dislikes, return inside and snuggle up with a mug of your favourite beverage. It's now time to sit down and work through your lists. Just read over them and highlight those 'dislikes' you feel most strongly about and also those 'likes' that really excite you. From your list of dislikes there are bound to be a number of things or features that you cannot simply get rid of. For example, you may not like the fact that there's a main road running outside your property and that you suffer from traffic noise as well as pollution. Obviously you're not going to be able to rush out and eradicate the road, but what you will be able to do with your design is work on ways of masking or at least minimising the road's presence so it doesn't impact on you as much.

WHAT NEEDS TO BE DISGUISED?

Your final list should include anything you don't like about your garden but you can't really get rid of it. For example, in the corner plot garden I mentioned earlier, we had a most annoying street light, which would shine directly into our bedroom at night, at times making sleep almost impossible. When I contacted our local council about the environmental impact that light pollution was having on our lives they weren't interested in listening to our complaint. That was some years ago and hopefully light pollution is now taken more seriously, but in any event I highlight this as an example of factors that can affect the enjoyment of your home, but which are outside your direct control. The secret to good garden design is to work on minimising their impact and by doing so remove the offending feature as a focus of attention. When the street lighting interfered with our enjoyment of the property, I created a planting scheme especially tall to reduce as much as possible the street light against our bedroom window, but which would allow daylight through. I achieved this with a mixture of phormiums and tall grasses. The positive thing was that at night when it was particularly windy, we'd be lulled to sleep by the restful noise of the grasses rustling in the wind.

YOUR THREE LISTS

By now you should have completed your three preliminary lists:

1. What you dislike about your garden – Dislikes.
2. What you like about your garden – Likes.
3. Features you dislike, but which are outside your control and will have to be disguised in some way – Disguise.

Dislikes, likes and disguises, are the three most important areas you're going to have to focus on. I've come across designers intent on creating a design without actually working out what it is that will make their clients really believe the designer has created their dream garden. Often it's something as simple as creating a garden that's easy to garden in. Or creating a garden that's easy to entertain in.

Don't forget the practicalities. When you're imagining your new garden you need to think not only about what aesthetic pleasure this garden will bring but also what will be the practical implications. For example, I've met homeowners who have asked me to build them a garden pond. When I've asked what they want the pond for, they've been surprised at the question. 'We just want a water feature,' is usually the common response. Or, 'We'd like to have a few fish.' The point is that if you're going to build a pond for fish then this introduces a number of further questions: What type of fish are you going to keep and how many? Did you know that in order to keep fish your pond should be of a certain size? The size is determined by the type of fish you intend to keep. So what might initially appear a relatively simple decision to make – ie, we'll have a pond – raises a number of further questions as to what you will be using the pond for.

This is why likes and dislikes are so important. For example, if you don't like or cannot stand the idea of having frogs and other waterlife hopping around your garden then you're better off not having a garden pond because this is the one thing that attracts them. Similarly, if you love wildlife you can create a garden rich in natural habitat to attract it. So spend some time on your likes, dislikes and disguise lists. These things really do form the foundations for your future garden plan. Nothing is worse than and more unattractive than a garden that's not planned and simply being created on a made-up-as-you-go-along basis. These gardens stand out a mile because generally speaking they will incorporate many or all of the seven deadly sins of amateur garden design.

◆ TIP ◆

Good garden design is all out information gathering. Record as much information as you can about your own needs and those of your household. Once you have done this you're ready to start work on your design.

◆ CHECKLIST ◆

- ◆ The first stage in designing your new garden is to work out your needs.

- ◆ The three areas of needs you should concentrate on are: your practical needs, the practical needs of those who live in your household and your inspirational needs.

- ◆ In addition to identifying your needs, you need to identify what you like about your present garden. The things you like will be those features you will retain in your new garden design.

- ◆ You also need to work out what you don't like about your existing garden. For example, it may be something simple like an ugly dilapidated garden shed, which you can get rid of when creating your new garden.

- ◆ There will also be things that you won't like about your existing garden, but you cannot easily get rid of them. For example, a road running immediately outside your home which brings with it traffic noise and fumes. Obviously, there's little you can do about this, so this is an area where you will have to work at disguising when it comes to working on your new design.

- ◆ Most gardeners' pet hates revolve around sensory things. For example, things we see, smell, hear, feel and touch. By identifying your own pet hate lists, you can work at either eradicating those things that annoy you or disguising them.

- ◆ It's important to gather all the information discussed in this chapter before starting work on your design. Information gathering is arguably the most important step in the design process.

3

IDENTIFYING POTENTIAL AND OPPORTUNITY

SEEING YOUR GARDEN AS A DESIGNER WOULD

Provided you've followed the exercises in Chapters 1 and 2, you should now have the following information recorded either in your Garden Journal or elsewhere:

1. Your completed needs lists.
2. Lists of those features in your present garden arrangement that you like, which means you'll want to keep them, those you don't like and can easily get rid of when creating your new garden, and finally those things you don't like but have to keep and will need to be disguised in some way.
3. An idea, rough or otherwise, of how much time and money you have available to spend on this project.

The next stage in the process is to start looking at your own garden as a garden designer would. The first step here is to identify areas where you can make simple improvements and those areas that offer the greatest potential. For example, at the moment you might have a wonderfully sunny spot in your garden that you could easily transform into another seating area.

IDENTIFYING POTENTIAL

Using either the notes you've already made about your garden during the sensory walk exercise or your lists of likes and dislikes, ask yourself if there is anything glaringly obvious that you can do to your garden that would make an instant improvement.

Is there anything glaringly obvious that can you do to your garden that would make an instant improvement? For example, I visited a regular client of ours one afternoon for a pre-booked hedge trim. As I was cutting the front hedge, she drove up the short driveway in her car, stopped and then climbed out onto the grass. Unfortunately the original house builder had made the driveway too narrow – a common problem by all accounts – and my client had to continually step on the lawn, which did nothing for the lawn and not a lot for her humour, especially when the grass was wet. I suggested to her having the driveway broadened to allow greater access. She told me she'd thought of this a number of times but the quotes for doing it were out of her budget.

I noticed that her side path had been laid using crazy paving, which she liked. I suggested that we create a small semicircle of similar crazy paving which we'd then simply tack on to the driveway and follow around so that it softened the hard edge of the driveway and gave an additional hard standing for her to step out on, as well as an additional area for her to put her pots. We agreed a price and the improvement was instant. No more stepping onto wet grass and the new hard standing area blended in with the crazy paving pathway.

◆ TIP ◆

The most successful method for identifying simple improvements is to question everything in your garden as to how suitable or user-friendly it is.

QUESTION EVERYTHING

The trick here is to first look at the practical aspects of your garden. For example, ask yourself what one thing you could do to make your garden more enjoyable. Look for the little things you could do. In my experience it's often the simplest of changes that can have the most impact. I've seen homeowners spend thousands of pounds having a new patio laid and the first thing their friends notice when they visit the garden isn't the new patio but the fact that the awful holly bush that attacked them everytime they visited had finally been got rid of.

We'll look at what's involved in getting proportion right in more detail shortly, but now is a good time to have a look at what I call the living areas of your garden – footpaths, driveways, patios, ponds, fences, etc. – and check them for size.

Ask yourself as you walk around:

◆ Is your patio large enough to cater for the sort of entertaining or family eating out that you'd like to do in your garden?

◆ If you're planning to have regular summer barbecues, is there already an area available for your barbecue that is close to the kitchen, or will you have to create a new one?

◆ Do you really need that old garden shed?

◆ Have you enough storage room in your existing shed to house all your gardening tools, so that they're easy to get out when you want to use them?

◆ Do you need a greenhouse (useful for extending the growing season and over-wintering certain plants), or do you want to get rid of the one you already have because you cannot see yourself using it and the space it's taking up could be better utilised?

◆ Are you tired of replacing or repairing fence panels and would you prefer to replace the whole fence with either something more solid like a wall, or something green like a living hedge?

◆ Have you got somewhere you can keep unsightly bins out of sight and away from the main garden living area?

EXERCISE

Drawing up a list of instant improvements

The benefit of drawing up a provisional list of instant improvements is that when it comes to working on your design you won't be faced with that awful blank paper stage, which makes it impossible to get anywhere. During my workshops I never actually get down to the real garden design until everybody has got some nice big lists worked up. It doesn't matter whether or not at this stage you can afford these improvements in terms of time and money, just get it all down. It'll loosen up your mind and get those creative juices flowing. So from now on I want you to start looking at your garden as a professional would: What can I do here? What improvements could I make there? Do I really need a great big shed at the bottom of the garden? Couldn't that area be turned into a sandpit for the children or grandchildren? Questions, keeping asking them. Why is that shrub there? Wouldn't it be better somewhere closer to the house so I can admire its beauty, smell its fragrance or touch its foliage every time I pass?

◆ TIP ◆

Successful garden design isn't about creating the next wonders of the world. It's about creating an outdoor living space that fits your needs and your lifestyle. Stress is something you leave at the garden gate whenever you arrive home.

HOW TO CARRY OUT A SIMPLE BUT EFFECTIVE SURVEY OF YOUR GARDEN

If you've already completed the above outdoor exercises, you're already halfway through your survey. If you haven't already got around to completing the outdoor dislikes, likes and what you can change a bit, I recommend you do so before going any further. It's an important part of the survey process and if you do nothing else but what I've previously recommended you're well on the way to a successful garden design.

THE ROUGH SKETCH AND MEASURE UP METHOD

No doubt this method will be frowned upon by garden design purists and professionals everywhere, but this is now the method I use because it works for me and is simple to do. I don't really see the point in getting bogged down with complicated survey mechanisms when you could be out there having fun redesigning and creating your new garden.

Equipment you'll need

You will need the following equipment to survey your garden:

1. Pencil, paper and an eraser.
2. A compass.
3. Builder's measuring tape.
4. Soil testing kit, which you can buy at most garden centres.

How to create your survey drawing

1. Divide your garden up into separate areas

If you only have a relatively small back garden, then you won't need to divide it up into areas. However, if surrounding your house you have a front garden, side garden and rear garden then my advice would be to divide your garden up into those three distinct areas and create a separate survey for each. Obviously, if you're only planning to redesign one area of your garden, then you only need to survey the area you're working on.

Make a rough drawing of each area of your garden. If your front garden is long and narrow, simply draw its outline on your pad. Make sure you include the outline of your property in each drawing.

2. Determine the aspect of each area

This is where your compass comes in handy. Simply stand in your front garden and work out the different aspects. For example, is your front garden south-facing? If it is this will mean that it will get lots of sunshine compared to other areas of your garden. Now work out your side garden's aspect and the aspect of your rear garden.

Determining the aspect of your garden will become useful when deciding on what plants and shrubs you should include in your new garden. For example, if you know that your front garden is south-facing and thus sunny, you're going to want to include lots of sun-loving plants. If your rear garden is north-facing, which will mean it will get the least amount of sunshine, then you're going to have to choose plants and shrubs that enjoy a shady or cooler environment.

Record your findings in your notebook.

3. Make a structure inventory of your present garden
Note on your drawing the position of any existing structures, for example:

◆ sheds
◆ greenhouses
◆ garages
◆ bin sheds
◆ compost areas

Include also the position of any outdoor services such as outdoor taps, drains, manholes, etc.

4. Record, measure and describe all of your property's boundaries and hard features
Draw in all your property boundaries and note what they are made of. For example, on one side of your property you may have a hedge, which we call a 'living boundary', and at the front of your property you may have a wall or fence. Of course you could also have a wall or fence immediately behind a hedge.

Using your measuring tape, measure the length of each boundary. If you have a particularly dense boundary, for example a densely planted hedge or border, then you should roughly measure the width of this as it will be useful when planning any additional planting.

Pencil in the outlines of all your pathways, patios, gates, driveway areas, etc. and include their measurements in your drawing. Include both the length and width of these features.

5. Record the position of existing planted areas such as borders and trees

Add the positions of any trees and draw an outline of your existing garden's borders. Try if you can to copy the shape of the border perimeters. For example, if you have a long straight border, simply draw a straight line, but if your borders are curved then try to replicate the shape.

6. Note any obvious problem areas

For example, if you have an area of your garden which is particularly damp or prone to waterlogging then note its position on your drawing. Or if you have an area of lawn that doesn't seem to grow very well perhaps because it's shaded by a tree or building line, then note this as well.

7. Include your dislikes

Even though you're planning to get rid of some features, you still need to include them in your survey drawing. Remember that this drawing is an overview of how your garden is at this moment in time, as opposed to how you'd like it to look once you've redesigned it.

8. Record any changes of levels

Note any changes of levels that might be immediately apparent in your garden. Record also the position of any steps or sloping pathways.

When measuring slopes a garden designer or landscape gardener will use an instrument known as a laser level to take various readings. Unless you're actually planning to remove any existing slopes or change the structure of your garden it's unlikely that you will need to record the slopes in such great detail. If you are planning to remove slopes or build structures on or into existing slopes then I recommend you seek the advice of a landscape gardener as this sort of garden construction work requires a qualified specialist.

9. Record all the other measurements

The final job is to pencil in all the outstanding measurements. For example, if you have a lawn area then it's a good idea to include its measurements in your survey drawing.

◆ TIP ◆

Don't worry at this stage about straight lines or working to scale. All you're aiming to do here is get a rough sketch of your garden in your notepad.

THE 'WHERE AND WHAT' OF GARDEN DESIGN

You've now completed the first of the two Ws – this being the *where*. In other words, you've jotted down where everything is. The next *W* you have to address is the *what* – what will grow in your garden? By this I mean getting a greater understanding of what makes up your garden in terms of soil, conditions, aspect, etc.

Shrubs and plants are a bit like people in that they too have needs. For example, they'll need water, light, food, etc. The basics that keep every living thing growing. But in addition, individual plants and shrubs will have specific needs in that for some to grow successfully they'll require lots of sunshine (sun-lovers), while others will be pleased relaxing in a nice shady corner (shade-tolerant plants).

SOIL AND CLIMATE ANALYSIS

Don't be put off by the somewhat austere and potentially technical and tedious-sounding undertaking of soil and climate analysis. Like the rough sketch and measurement method introduced above, I advise a similar approach when it comes to working out what type of soil you have in your garden. Don't get bogged down in technicalities. All you need is a rough but generally accurate idea of what growing potential your garden holds.

Aspect

If you've already completed the previous survey exercises you will have worked out what aspect your garden has. For example, have you a south-facing, sun-drenched garden or a relatively cold and possibly damp north-facing garden? Aspect is one of those things that you can do little about. It's impossible to turn your house around so that it faces the right way! Instead, the trick here is to work out what you have and then fill it with shrubs and plants that thrive in such an aspect. But before you do this, you need to have an idea of what type of soil your garden has.

Essentially, there are three main types of soil:

1. Sandy.
2. Clay.
3. Loam.

Sandy soil

As the name suggests, sandy soil is very gritty and light. It has a similar texture to the type of soil you'd find near the seaside. Easy to dig, it allows water to drain away without causing flooding or puddles, but lacks any real solid structure. If you've sandy soil, you'll need to improve its texture and structure by adding large amounts of organic material.

Clay soil

Most of us will be familiar with clay soil, which is very sticky when wet. You know you've got clay when you're outside in your garden in the wet weather and it all sticks to the soles of your Wellington boots in great big clods. The problem with clay soil is that when it rains it doesn't allow the water to run through it and you get lots of puddles and flooding. Then when the weather is dry, the soil texture takes on all the attributes of concrete. Clay soil can be improved by adding sand and grit, which help break up the structure and allow air and water to sieve through it.

Loam

Loam is every gardener's dream. Loamy soil is lovely and soft, crumbly and rich. Water is retained in it without flooding and no matter how hot the weather it won't go like concrete. You don't need to do a great deal to improve loamy soil apart from adding some compost in autumn or spring.

In reality, most gardens will have a combination of all three soil types. Depending on what's already been happening in your garden, you may well find that some areas are nice and loamy (usually where veggies have been growing) while others are very clayey. Whatever soil type you have don't despair, as you really can work to improve the fertility and texture of your soil.

EXERCISE – TEST YOUR SOIL

It is now time now to determine what type or types of soil you have in your garden. You can do this by using the above information and also by using a soil testing kit to determine your garden's pH levels.

Soil testing kits

There are a number of ways you can test your soil and I recommend that as part of your testing you purchase a small soil testing kit available from most garden centres or online gardening retailers. For a relatively small investment you get a fairly accurate soil analysis. All you have do is follow the instructions on the packet. Generally speaking, you should test soil from a number of different sites within your garden as the soil type could vary from place to place.

Another useful and mostly reliable method of working out your soil type is to look at what's growing successfully in your neighbourhood. Don't just limit your observations to neighbours' gardens but look at the natural growth as well. For example, if you live out in the countryside you should look to the natural growths of hedgerows and any garden areas. Some areas near our town have huge belts of rhododendrons and azaleas, which indicate a high acidity in the soil and of course mean that these shrubs will do well in your garden also. Don't be afraid to ask your neighbours, particularly those whose gardens are flush with vibrant foliage and rich planting schemes, for their experiences with local climatic conditions. Your independent local garden centre or plant nursery is also a good point of call for information on local growing conditions, provided of course you can find a horticulturist as opposed to simply retail staff with no gardening experience.

Your local newspaper can also be full of useful knowledge as many papers have regular gardening columns usually written by local gardeners. These columns can contain a wealth of information about local growing conditions and anything peculiar to where you live.

A visit to your local library and council offices can also pay dividends, in that they will have leaflets and guides on local gardens that are open to the public. If you have any of these gardens near where you live, then make sure you visit them not just with a view to getting ideas for your new garden but also to have a good look at what's growing there. Open gardens usually have knowledgeable, skilled gardeners who in my experience are only too pleased to answer visitors' questions and offer advice and help.

Points of information for your soil analysis include:

◆ Soil testing kits available from garden centres and online retailers.
◆ What you see growing locally.
◆ Talking to your neighbours, especially those who have an obvious flare for gardening.
◆ Speaking to local nurserymen or plants persons asking for advice on local growing conditions.
◆ Gardening columns in local newspapers.
◆ Visiting any local gardens that are open to the public.

Climatic conditions

Local climatic conditions will depend on a number of factors. For example, I live in the south-east of England and my garden is only a few hundred yards from the sea. One of the benefits of living here is that we enjoy living in an area regarded as having the most sunshine in the UK. Certainly this is an advantage not just when it comes to cultivating and growing shrubs and plants, but also the relatively good weather means we get to enjoy our gardens more than in other areas that are generally dominated by higher rainfall and are less sunny. But the drawbacks of living here mean that we suffer from at times prolonged ferocious winds that cause much damage to tender plants. With lower rainfall, we seem at the moment to have perpetual hosepipe bans and our gardens are prone to being frazzled by the sun one week and the winds the following week.

So there is no perfect weather climate for the gardener. Again, what's important is that you recognise the potentially damaging effects that climate can have on your future garden's welfare and put in place sufficient preventative measures to reduce the impact of any harsh conditions.

In the main, few shrubs and plants will thrive where they are exposed and generally most will thank you for a nice sheltered spot. Therefore when surveying your garden remember to take note of the climatic conditions local to you. For example, if you're living in an area where your garden will be exposed to frequent high winds, you're going to need to incorporate into your plan as many wind-resistant or wind-tolerant shrubs and plants as you can and/or preferably look at ways of sheltering your garden.

Where I come from originally on the west coast of Ireland, the winds can be harsh to say the least and often the driving rain is salty from the sea – all of which takes its toll on the gardeners' hard work. That said, my father manages to grow all sorts of unusual tropical shrubs and trees in his garden as well as a wide range of plants that wouldn't usually be considered suitable for these gardening conditions. However, because of his ingenuity and determination in creating natural sheltered areas in his garden, he manages to grow whatever he wants. So while relatively inhospitable climatic conditions shouldn't necessarily restrict your planting plans, you will need to consider constructing your garden so it affords the necessary shelter.

GARDEN SURVEY NOW COMPLETE

By now you should have completed your garden survey and recorded the following information:

1. Your lists of likes, dislikes and what needs to be disguised in your new garden.
2. Your garden's soil and climatic analysis.
3. A survey drawing of your garden.

INFORMATION GATHERING PROCESS NOW COMPLETE

You've now completed the information gathering process, which as I said previously is arguably the most important stage in the design process.

By now you should have a clear idea of where you're going in terms of your project. For example, you know now what features in your garden you'll be getting rid of as well as those that need to be disguised. You've also gathered some very useful and necessary information about your present garden in terms of its size, layout, soil and climatic conditions.

In the next chapter, I'm going to show you how you can put all this work to use to plan your first garden.

◆ CHECKLIST ◆

- ◆ Make sure you complete your survey before moving on to designing your garden.

- ◆ You also need to determine what type of soil you have in your garden as this information will be very useful when deciding on what to plant and where to plant it.

- ◆ Climatic conditions will vary depending on where you live. For example, if you live by the coast then your climatic conditions will be very different to someone who lives in the city. Identifying the climatic conditions local to you is important as this will determine what plants and shrubs are suitable for your new garden.

- ◆ Don't get too bogged down with the technical aspects of the survey drawing. While you should try to be as accurate as you can with your measurements, a rough drawing and measurements are better than nothing.

4

PRINCIPLES OF CREATIVE GARDEN DESIGN

WHAT MAKES A TRULY MAGICAL GARDEN?

Some time ago I received a phone call from a prospective client who began by explaining that she had no interest in gardening. She told me that until now her husband, a keen gardener, had undertaken all the work but illness and age had meant that he was no longer able to carry on. So the solution was to find a gardener to work their garden. She pointed out that was her husband's view. Her own opinion was that the whole area would be better off covered with concrete.

Given her comments in relation to concreting, I was initially somewhat reluctant to go there as I didn't feel that the job on offer was something I'd be interested in. I'd learnt over the years that when prospective clients talk unenthusiastically about their gardens, especially when they see them as nothing more than a necessary inconvenience, rarely were they ever willing to pay the rates that I demanded for working on a large garden.

Usually the client saw me as too expensive and I viewed them as having unrealistic expectations as to what it would cost to turn their garden into something beautiful. So with this somewhat negative view of it all, I turned up late one afternoon to meet my prospective client.

As soon as I drew up alongside the front of the house and saw the open-plan garden, I changed my mind. Any negative thoughts I had gave way to the wow factor that only comes with working on such a brilliant garden.

Although somewhat staid and unadventurous in appearance, the front garden really took me. The two towering conifers standing guard at the main entrance were magnificent, as was the lush conifer-based perimeter hedging. My mood lifted as I knocked the door and a smiling woman waved me in. 'Hopefully you can help us,' she said, leading me through the house and into the back garden where I stood for a moment open-mouthed at the splendid view that unfolded in front of me. In my opinion they didn't get much better than this and after a brief walk around the garden we managed to agree a regular maintenance fee together with a one-off payment to get the garden back to its original glory.

So what made this gardening so magical?

Well for a start the garden flowed. There were no unseemly joins of any description. Every feature of the garden worked and earned its keep as it should, but the most striking feature of all was that although this was a relative large garden – certainly compared to newbuilds today it was huge – everything was in proportion. There was no evidence at all of any of my seven amateur garden design sins and the borders were full of interesting foliage and shrubs with not a single bedding plant in evidence anywhere.

The garden was planned in such a way that there was something interesting and inspiring to look at whatever the season.

This was a garden that changed with the seasons without the need for emptying borders of annual bedding and replacing them with more. I'm not knocking bedding plants here, simply that this garden worked with nature and consequently everything ran at a natural pace with little or no human intervention needed. The only requirement was for a gardener to keep it maintained, which considering the size of the garden was an enormous task in itself.

THE IMPORTANCE OF MAKING YOUR GARDEN LOOK NATURAL

A garden is made up of a variety of living and non-living features, all of which must be able to come together to create something magical and unique.

When it comes to what makes a garden truly magical, I believe it's one where everything appears natural and uncontrived. In my client's garden the planting schemes blended in seamlessly with the lawn area, which was of a sufficient size and in proportion to the rest of the garden and house. Border hedging was of the right density and height. When I stood on the patio area outside the French doors I was awe-struck not by the size of the garden, but by its togetherness. Everything worked! Even the secondary hedge at the rear of the garden with the rose-covered central entrance served to create a gardener's working area, tucked out of sight of the main house. Here was an area for composting, and a garden shed large enough to take all the tools, mowers and equipment and still leave room to get in and out without having to clamber over everything else.

I spent two gloriously happy years working in this garden until the pressure of work commitments and a change in the homeowner's personal circumstances forced us to part company. I still drive past the garden and visit from time to time and I can honestly say that the garden has never lost any of its magical charm.

Magical gardens are those that:

◆ Regardless of their size, complement the home they surround, rather than making it look too small or too large.
◆ Are seamless in every way. There are no rough edges or unfinished areas, and like in a top hotel or restaurant any unsightly areas are a closely guarded secret, their whereabouts known only to their owners/gardeners.
◆ They don't rely on seasonal replantings for colour and effect. Instead they change naturally with the seasons.
◆ Positively welcome visitors with ample seating areas, functional areas and navigate you gently through their beauty without the need for you to stoop, bow or otherwise protect yourself from overhanging branches or foliage.
◆ Are as much a pleasure to work in as they are to relax in.

This is by no means an exhaustive list, but I believe that every garden regardless of its size or aspect has the potential to be a truly magical garden.

INTRODUCING HARD AND SOFT FEATURES

As the names imply, hard features are those things in your garden that once installed are fixed or unmovable, for example patios, pathways, driveways, seating areas, etc, while soft features include lawn areas, planting areas, trees, borders, etc.

WHAT'S INVOLVED WHEN PLANNING HARD FEATURES?

In my experience it's most important when planning your first garden that you get the position and size of hard features right from the start, as to redo them at some later stage will not only be potentially very expensive but will also create a certain amount of unwanted disruption.

You should view hard features as you would the internal walls of your house. Once constructed they're somewhat immovable. The soft features are similar to the furnishings of your rooms. So pathways, walls, fences, etc. become the walls of your garden and the plants, shrubs, lawn area and water features become the furnishings. Obviously, just as with your home, there will only ever be a certain amount of space to accommodate everything. You don't need me to tell you how unpleasant, impractical and entirely frustrating a cluttered room can be, yet overcrowding is a common flaw in many garden designs. And rather than having a garden that looks inviting and inspiring, the result is more often stress-inducing. I once had a client who simply would not accept that she had planted her shrubs too close together, which resulted in many of them dying off. According to her, everything else was to blame.

Factors to consider when designing hard features:

◆ Choice of materials. You'll need to decide what type of materials you want to use for your hard features. For example, what sort of stone in terms of texture, colour, shape and size are you going to use for any new patio or pathways?

◆ Are the features that you're planning sympathetic with your property? For example, if you live in an old cottage and you want a raised decked area, how will this new feature blend in with the older property?

◆ Rather than going to the time and expense of constructing new hard features, could you possibly reuse or improve on existing structures?

MAKING USE OF YOUR SURVEY DRAWING AND INFORMATION

As you now have a sketched plan of your garden together with a survey and accompanying notes, you have all you need to get started on the main task of designing your garden.

When it comes to designing, start by using your lists.

When designing your garden, start working on the most obvious bits. For example, you've already worked out your lists of what's going, staying and what needs to be disguised. Next work out what you're going to add. Maybe you need additional seating space, an area for the children to play or a greenhouse to work in.

However, before you get stuck into working on your design, there are a number of factors that I'd like you to consider.

THE LOW-MAINTENANCE GARDEN

If you haven't the time or the inclination to spend lots of time gardening, then obviously the low-maintenance garden design is for you.

This is where your completed Lifestyle Questionnaire comes in, and one of the first and arguably the most important decisions about your future garden needs to be addressed: How much time have you actually got to garden? And do you actually like gardening?

Lots of people I've come across have started off at my workshops saying how much they love gardening, but when I ask them whether or not they enjoy spending their Saturday mornings or Friday evenings on their knees weeding they change their mind. Of course not all gardening is a chore, and certainly whatever your future garden plan you should try to create a garden in which you can minimise if not eradicate the need for on-your-knees weeding, but nevertheless try to be as realistic as you can.

As a professional working gardener, I've spent much of my life tending to others' gardens. Work that I've enjoyed. However, there is one thing that I will never undertake for any client and that's weeding. So when a client approaches me with a weed problem I basically sell them a garden makeover with the aim of eradicating the need for weeding.

How is this achieved? Simply by treating the areas that are prone to weeds with a denser and more invasive planting scheme. It's a simple natural solution to weeds. That's why I'm never keen on borders that rely entirely on seasonal bedding for effect, as these areas will always be prone to weeds at various times. For instance, at the start of the season when you plant your bedding plants they will be significantly smaller than later in the season and thus while waiting for them to mature, weeds will love nothing more than to fill the gaps. Then at the end of the season or when the first frosts arrive, your summer bedding overnight falls to the ground to be replaced by a whole variety of perennial weeds.

By choosing a planting scheme that doesn't over rely on twice-yearly border clearances or replantings, you'll soon have mature shrubbery that will not only give you the wonderful benefit of all-year round colour and interest, but just as importantly, there will be no soil space left for those dreaded weeds to grow up.

Thus, what might appear on the face of it to be a high-maintenance solution – to plant more shrubs than you normally would – can actually be a low-maintenance solution.

A low-maintenance solution doesn't always deliver on its promises.

Much of my work as a gardener comes about somewhat sadly as a result of someone's change in personal circumstances. Similarly to the earlier example of the lady whose gardening husband had a stroke and was no longer able to garden, I had a call from another lady who had lived together all her life with her brother who had sadly passed away. Just like the other lady, this woman had no real interest in gardening, but wanted her home to look as presentable and as interesting as it was when her brother had been alive. The solution I offered her was to suggest she employ a jobbing gardener to tend to her garden once a week, as it was what I would consider a high-maintenance garden. She rejected this idea on the basis that it would cost too much and instead employed another 'landscape gardener' to redesign her garden so that it became low-maintenance. I cringed when she told me of his plans to chop down the beautiful weeping willow trees that adorned her garden. And if this was not bad enough, the further plans included taking up the front lawn and replacing it with a layer of 'decorative shingle' with a paved area for her pots to sit on. As you'll know from my earlier list of deadly sins, this sort of garden will never be inspiring and ultimately, I believe, resembles a grave.

Despite my best efforts she went ahead with the plan and in a matter of a few short weeks her once beautiful, interesting and inspirational garden was transformed into a 'low-maintenance garden'. As the garden of one of my regular clients was directly opposite I got to see the full horror of a once-beautiful garden butchered in the name of low maintenance.

Although the new garden could hardly be called attractive, it had on first viewings satisfied the lady's requirements in as much as she wouldn't have to undertake any heavy gardening work. Certainly there was no longer a lawn to cut and the once-flourishing borders – prone to occasional weeding over – were now safely buried under a 2mm layer of cheap stone. But problems began to appear a couple of months later when the weeds seemingly appeared overnight. The lady was distraught. Whereas before she only had the borders to contend with, it now appeared that everywhere was covered. She asked me to have a look, which I reluctantly did, and in a matter of seconds literally uncovered the problem – the contractor had not put any weed-preventative barrier down, instead laying the shingle over the bare soil. I'll show you later what preparations are needed to stop this sort of thing from happening, but for this woman it was all too late and despite her best efforts the contractor never returned to put things right and the whole garden spiralled into decline.

What started off as a low-maintenance solution became anything but. Even with proper preparations and the inclusion of weed-preventative membrane barriers, you can still expect to have to weed your shingled area. This is because the birds will drop their seeds in the shingle and wind and rain will distribute a certain amount of sand and soil which over a period of time will prove fertile ground for weeds. Perhaps not in huge numbers, but they'll arrive all the same.

So if either you don't like gardening or you know as a result of completing your Lifestyle Questionaire that you're going to have little time to tend to your garden, then obviously you want a low-maintenance garden solution. But please don't think that the only options open to you are to concrete, pave or shingle over your garden. There are far better, more interesting and inspirational solutions that you can introduce into your design.

THE GREEN LOW-MAINTENANCE ALTERNATIVE

If you're still caught up on the idea of shingling over everything, remember that even if you don't get the weeds your shingle garden will need raking to keep it even and looking at its best. Did you know that Japanese gardens are raked daily to maintain their wonderful appearances and shapes?

An alternative is to keep a lawn area, which only requires cutting once a week during the relatively short growing season – April to September – and the benefit is you get all year-round colour. Green is also an extremely cooling colour and a lush lawn can be a welcome relief on a hot sticky day.

So low maintenance doesn't mean boring. Neither should it limit your garden plans.

THE HIGH-MAINTENANCE GARDEN

If you love gardening and have lots of spare time, then a high-maintenance garden can be the perfect solution. Again a common misconception is that a high-maintenance garden is one in which you have lots of tall, long hedges, trees, and things that require continual pruning. On the contrary. I know lots of gardeners who have what would in every respect be generally accepted as low-maintenance gardens but which have areas devoted to their favourite type of gardening. For example, for some this will be incorporating a wonderful vegetable garden or fruit tree garden. Others will simply have a greenhouse where they spend all year tending to produce a certain type of plant, shrub or even tree.

So if you have lots of time available to garden and love gardening, it's still worth sitting down now and working out what type of gardening you enjoy most. Growing under glass? Vegetable and fruit production? Raising rare plants or producing your own hybrids? Or just simply general gardening where you love every aspect, including finding weeding therapeutic. I know lots of gardeners who take a great delight from weeding borders. It's all gardening and everyone has different pleasures.

EXERCISE – A LOW- OR HIGH-MAINTENANCE GARDEN?

It's time now for you to decide what type of garden you want. Low maintenance where you spend as much time as possible relaxing and enjoying your outdoor space, or high maintenance where you love every minute of your spare time gardening.

Whatever you decide it doesn't need to be final but by making an early decision you'll find that planning your new garden becomes much easier as you now have a certain *objective* to work towards. Up until now you've simply been planning your first garden. You've now changed your focus from simply designing a garden to planning one that fits your lifestyle, and that's important. Too many gardens are created without ever addressing their owners' needs in terms of time available and lose sight of the enjoyment factor. If you don't like general gardening but would like a great garden then that's absolutely achievable.

GETTING TO GRIPS WITH DESIGNING A SMALL OR LARGE GARDEN

The next stage in the design process is to consider some of the factors that will affect or impact on the design of your garden based on its overall size. Obviously the advantage of designing a small garden is that ultimately it will be easier to create than a larger garden. However, as you'll see, a potential disadvantage is that you'll have to squeeze all of your needs into a very small space – a difficult task in itself.

DESIGNING A SMALL GARDEN

My present garden is a courtyard garden. A tiny area surrounded by flint-stone walls on three sides with a boundary neighbouring fence completing its perimeter. It's certainly small and a garden that a few years ago I would never have considered as suitable for me as I've always identified myself as one of those high-maintenance gardeners who enjoy nothing more than pottering around a greenhouse when it's wet, cold or windy and when the weather's kinder working borders or vegetables plots. However, a few years ago I expanded my hobbies to rediscover the pleasures of sailing, kayaking and cycling. It was then that I found our relatively large garden becoming a strain on myself and my partner's free time.

Having worked as professional gardeners all week, we'd escape to spend weekends exploring the coast on our small sailing boat. Even if the weather was terrible we'd get away on our boat. It didn't take long for our garden to show signs of neglect and there came a point when I dreaded returning home late on Sunday nights to find more once-loved shrubs or plants either blown ragged by the wind or scorched and dry from the sun. The greenhouse, once a home to thriving herb production, became a sorry, embarrassing sight and I ended up giving away treasured plants to neighbours, friends and anyone who would have them.

When we decided to sell our home, we sat down and discussed what we wanted from our new house. Deciding on the house wasn't difficult. We wanted something with period character, close to the sea and as near to the town centre as possible. Yet deciding on our ideal garden proved a nightmare.

As a child I had always dreamt of having a big garden. I'd never really given much thought to the house, but the garden was always in my dreams. Big and beautiful with lawns, herbs and vegetable areas surrounded by dense hedging where everything and everyone outside couldn't be heard or seen. Obviously, trying to find a house either in or near any town centre with a large garden is impossible. Or if they exist you have to be incredibly wealthy, well-connected or both to be able to buy one. The choice had to be made. Should we buy the house we wanted and accept that we'd either get a tiny garden, no garden or worse – a communal garden complete with shared furniture and fish pond?

After mulling it over for a while, we both decided that we'd actually welcome a house with a small garden. After all, we really were struggling to cope with the large garden we had so it would be a relief to enjoy a smaller garden with its low-maintenance appeal. Thus it was that we purchased an Edwardian house complete with its charming courtyard garden. When we viewed the property the garden was full of tall plants, shrubs and pots. But when the day came for us to move in we were shocked to find that the vendors had taken all of it with them, leaving us with a vacant characterless space.

The first thing on what turned out to be a long list of 'to do' items was for me to come up with a design for the courtyard garden. Although I had in the past worked in many small gardens, I had never really designed one and as I began to work my way through my design I discovered that designing a small garden is far more difficult than planning for a larger garden.

If yours is a small garden – or perhaps a part of it is small, for example a tiny front garden and a relatively large back garden, which isn't uncommon – I want to flag up certain problems that face your future design.

Some factors you will need to consider:

1. A poor design really stands out.
2. Getting the practicalities right.
3. Impact of colour.
4. Creating your own private space.

A poor design really stands out

An obvious problem with a small garden is that you have limited space, but a more pressing problem is that it's likely that all of your rear windows will look out onto your garden. In our house, the kitchen takes up the entire width of the house, which means that it looks into the garden. The benefit of this is that when we entertain friends and family in the kitchen-diner, we can use the garden as an extended living space.

Unlike larger gardens, where you can break up the site into various 'rooms' or areas, you cannot do this with a small garden. Your design must work and deliver on your requirements. Cram too much in and you'll end up with a claustrophobic mess. Too little and it'll forever look unfinished. Hence you really do need to spend more time planning your small garden than you do creating it.

Getting the practicalities right

Personally I've never wanted to live in a show garden. It's all very well looking at those wonderful, inspirational gardens on television programmes but day-to-day life wouldn't fare too well in many of them. For example, we have two relatively large dogs who I believe should be able to relax and enjoy themselves in our garden after long walks on the beach.

Wherever possible I like to dry clothes outdoors, which means I've installed a pull-out clothes line that's only visible when it's being used. Some people I know believe that the sight of washing on a line in a court-yard garden the size of ours spoils the overall affect. However, I believe the opposite to be true. Not only is drying clothes outdoors good for the environment, it's also making good practical use of outdoor space. Which in my view is what good garden design is all about.

As I said earlier, we like to entertain. Nothing beats a house full of friends at any time of the year and our parties always spread out to the garden. Thus our garden, small as it may be, has to accommodate many varied needs.

A common design solution for small, courtyard gardens is to fill the floor area with pots and containers. Obviously this wouldn't work in our court-yard as we need the floor space. So when planning our garden I had to consider and ensure that the long list of practical needs could be squeezed in. It took planning and lots of revisions of my original ideas and designs, but in the end I came up with a design that gives us a beautiful garden view from our kitchen and a practical, restful and inspirational garden to work in.

IMPACT OF COLOUR IN A SMALL GARDEN

Never underestimate the impact of colour in a small garden space. If you love red then beware that this colour has the effect of bringing everything closer to you and can also if not tempered with additional planting of cooler shades, for example plants and shrubs with blues and greens, you may end up creating a somewhat stressful garden.

My own courtyard garden at home is surrounded by two beautiful tall flint walls and a close-boarding boundary fence separating my garden from that of our neighbour's cottage. It's a small area and during the summer months a sun trap. So I've been careful in choosing a planting scheme that creates a cool, calm garden area.

Some of the shrubs and plants that I have used in my own courtyard garden to create a calming effect include:

◆ To disguise the wooden close-boarding fencing I have planted a griselinia hedge. Griselinia is evergreen, which means it keeps its leaves all year. As it's salt-tolerant and able to resist wind, it's ideal for our seaside location. It also creates a thick, dense hedge which reduces noise from neighbouring properties as well as introducing lots of green into our small space, thus creating a cooling effect.

◆ On one of the flint walls I have a magnificent wisteria. Although wisteria loses its leaves over the winter and during this period looks uninteresting, it makes up for it come spring when the leaves return and by early summer it blooms with the most striking purple flowers.

◆ In the damp shady corner I have a variety of hostas. Similar to the wisteria, these only really come into their own during late spring and summer and die back in the autumn, but the green and blue hues of their structured leaves create an instant calming effect. Hostas are ideal for damp, shady conditions and if like me you haven't got a water feature or pond they manage to give the impression that you do.

◆ In one corner I have planted a large variegated laurel, an acuba, which gives year-round colour and contrast, and softens the corner of the garden where the flint wall meets the wooden fence.

◆ Against the rear flint wall I have an abundance of honeysuckle. With its yellow flowers, green leaves and wonderful aroma, it makes an excellent climber.

When it comes to painting any hard features such as fences or walls, you'll need to make sure that the colour you choose creates a sense of space as opposed to bringing everything closer. Therefore for the practical purpose of getting a good working design you may have to forego relying on your favourite colours and working with those that will give the best overall effect.

Creating your own private space

By their very nature town or small gardens are usually surrounded by other properties. Our house is part of an Edwardian terrace and we've houses directly behind us who, when we moved in, were able to see directly into our courtyard garden. With my design I needed to create a sense of privacy and serenity without insulting our new neighbours. There are a number of ways this can be achieved without simply raising the fence or building higher walls. Again bear this problem in mind when it comes to your new design. If you are overlooked, you'll need to address this in your plan.

WHAT CAN HELP WHEN DESIGNING LARGER GARDENS

If you have a large garden, don't despair. Designing on a larger scale can actually be far easier than coming up with design solutions for smaller spaces. The obvious downside to creating a new large garden is that not only will the project take considerably longer with much more disruption, but you're also going to have to think very carefully about budgets. In my experience, larger projects usually end up costing far more than anyone thought they would. An extra pathway here, or a bit more paved area there and a nice acer tree at the end of the garden and suddenly your costs are out of control. So if you have a large garden I'd recommend you tackle it this way:

◆ Decide now whether or not you actually need to redesign the whole garden in one attempt.

◆ Consider dividing your garden up into separate areas, which you should then prioritise. For example, it may be that the bottom area of your garden looks like a wilderness or is entirely barren. However, the area immediately outside your home has an acceptable level of features such as a good patio or a place to sit, entertain and enjoy the garden. While you might like and ultimately want a new patio or entertaining area and maybe a nice water feature, you should leave this until after you've tackled the area beyond.

◆ If you're unsure about where you should start, my advice would be to begin with the part of the garden that you're most likely to use. Although a matter of personal choice, I think it's important that in your initial garden design you create a garden that's comfortable to live in. Nothing is worse than having a beautifully manicured lawn with nowhere to sit and enjoy the view. Or if you have children you're going to have to prioritise your design to incorporate a safe and interesting area for them to play in and one where you can easily keep an eye on them.

◆ Beware of budget. I mentioned this earlier and I really do want to urge you to be cautious. In the past I've met many homeowners who had an entirely unrealistic view of how much it was all going to cost. Many work away under the impression that because they're doing the physical graft themselves, the whole thing can be done on a shoestring. Certainly you can make great savings by undertaking the heavy work yourself. However, I've lost count of the times I've been approached by DIYers offering me turfs, paving slabs, sand and even plants because they've managed to get their quantities wrong. Thes errors undoubtedly blow budgets and wipe out the potential savings of doing the work yourself. While you don't need to spend a fortune to transform your garden into something truly magical, you should prepare a realistic budget. If you're planning a new patio area, go to your local builder's merchant, grab some catalogues and a price list and work out some rough figures. Lawns aren't cheap either, even when you prepare and lay them yourself. So again be prepared to work out some initial figures and set a realistic, affordable budget.

◆ From here on, be on the lookout for bargains. Our local freebie weekly paper has a gardening section that's full of all sort of wonderful plants, shrubs and trees that are either available for a fraction of the cost you'd pay in a garden centre, or in many cases free to collect provided you're willing to go dig whatever it is up and cart it away. You can also source good-quality used tools in this way and save yourself fortunes. No doubt you can benefit from others overordering!

◆ CHECKLIST ◆

- ◆ When designing your garden, start with the obvious things. For example, what can be easily improved, removed or altered?

- ◆ Create a list of the features you will be including in your new garden that aren't already in existence.

- ◆ A magical garden is one that flows effortlessly, where everything works without appearing contrived or staged.

- ◆ Decide on whether you want a low- or high-maintenance garden.

- ◆ When designing a small garden you're going to have to work harder at getting the design right, as squeezing all your needs in a small space and making it work together requires some creative thinking.

- ◆ If your garden is large, consider dividing your project into separate areas. Prioritise where to start first and complete each area before moving onto the next.

- ◆ Start thinking about the budget. How much is it all going to cost? See how you can reduce your expenditure, for example by purchasing shrubs and plants from classified advertisements in your local paper as opposed to at garden centres.

5

DECIDING ON A STYLE FOR YOUR GARDEN AND FINALISING YOUR PLAN

CREATING A WORKING PLAN FOR YOUR NEW GARDEN

Until now you've been working on your Survey Drawing. This drawing is based on your existing garden. It's now time to use this drawing and the information you have gathered to draw a plan for your new garden.

Professional garden designers will usually create three separate plans for their clients as follows:

1. Functional Plan
2. Planting Plan
3. Master Plan.

Let's look at what's involved with each plan.

THE FUNCTIONAL PLAN

The Functional Plan is a *working plan* on which you get to play with your garden. With this plan you don't have to be too specific with measurements or positions or try to reconcile any snagging problems, for example how you will overcome a particular design problem. Instead a Functional Plan is one on which you can draw things, have a look at how they work on paper and erase whatever you're unhappy with.

Professional garden designers will draw up a Functional Plan from the notes they took during your initial meetings and after having referred to their Design Brief.

Rather than spend hours working on drawing to scale what they imagine the new garden might look like, they simply create a rough working drawing. This is the Functional Plan, which they take with them to their meetings with clients.

I'll show you how to create your own Functional Plan from the information you have already gathered in just a moment, but first let me tell you about the remaining two garden plans, which you may or may not need.

THE PLANTING PLAN

This plan will basically outline what you intend to do by way of planting arrangements. The easiest way to create your planting plan is to draw an outline of where your planting will be, including all border areas, and noting the locations of any trees on your garden plan. Then on a separate piece of paper or in your Garden Journal, list all the shrubs, plants and trees that you intend to introduce into your new garden.

THE MASTER PLAN

As the title suggests, a Master Plan is the final plan of your new garden, complete with every imaginable detail. The Master Plan created by a professional garden designer will include not just an overall plan of the garden in terms of where everything will be located, but also include information for whoever will be appointed to build the new garden. For example, were you hiring in a landscape gardener to create your patio area, water features, etc., they would need to see some plans of the size and dimensions of the features together with any special instructions as to what materials should be used when building them.

The Master Plan will be drawn to scale and will also include a number of views showing what your new garden will look like. For example, the designer would give you a drawing showing what the garden will look like when you look at it from outside your home.

Is a Master Plan necessary for planning your first garden?

The amount of work that goes into creating a Master Plan should never be underestimated. Neither should the skills and training needed to complete one. Even those with a relatively small garden will find that it takes hours to create complete and detailed scale drawings. My own view is that it's more important for you to spend your energies and enthusiasm creating your new garden than labour away with a pencil creating a brilliant drawing that you don't really need. Rather than spend time on a final Master Plan, my advice would be to create a working Functional Plan together with a Planting Plan. The disadvantage of this is that at the end of your project you will have a relatively rough around the edges plan of your new garden. But this book is more about helping you to plan and create your new garden than creating time-consuming plans that might never materialise. You'd be surprised at how many clients I've visited who have the most wonderful sets of expensively produced Master Plans that have never been created.

For the purposes of planning and creating your first garden, it's best to work with a Functional Plan.

Obviously your Functional Plan will need to be as accurate as possible in terms of measurements and details. But you won't have to go to the time and work of including every last detail to scale. Neither will you need to learn the relatively complicated drafting and illustrating techniques employed by professional garden designers to give perspective to their garden plans. After all, you're undertaking the project yourself and aren't simply giving the plans to someone else. This is your project and by the time you complete your planning, you're going to be very familiar with every existing and proposed detail of your new garden.

CREATING YOUR FUNCTIONAL PLAN

The easiest way to create your Functional Plan is to work with 'thumbnail sketches', which are simply small drawing plans of what your new garden is going to look like.

How big should your thumbnail sketches be?

Personally I like to make my thumbnail sketches as small as possible, and certainly no larger than A5 sized. Usually I try to make my sketches in my notebooks. However, depending on where I am and what I'm otherwise doing means that many of my best designs have been created on everything from the backs of envelopes and business cards to paper napkins. So don't get too caught up in how exact and professional your thumbnail sketch is going to look. The real benefit of creating thumbnail sketches is that they are simple to do – a bit like doodling – and you don't have to worry how you're going to fill otherwise daunting blank spaces without getting too hung up on detail.

When sketching your thumbnails you're going to need to refer back to the information gathered when you completed your garden survey. If like me you tend to read through a book like this first and then go back and read it again while working through the author's recommended exercises, then I'd still recommend you grab a piece of paper and start working up some thumbnail sketches.

What's the advantage of using thumbnails as opposed to scale drawings?

Without fail, at the beginning of each workshop someone will ask what is the advantage of creating thumbnail drawings over creating scale drawings that include every detail.

It's a perfectly sensible question. I always reply that the workshop – and this book – is about planning and creating your first garden as opposed to creating a scale drawing. The energy and time needed first to learn how to and then actually to create a perfect scale drawing is considerable and in my view unnecessary. Unless you're looking to use this project as an exercise at the start of a garden design career, you're better off concentrating on coming up with ideas and solutions that can be easily replicated on paper using simple drawings.

Thumbnail garden design sketches are the equivalent of the stick people drawings created by some artists. Thumbnails are a perfect way for anyone regardless of their artistic ability to put their ideas on paper without worrying about drawing techniques. Provided you work within your crucial measurements, these being the ones you took when completing your initial survey, then you're fine. You don't have to worry about calculating and apportioning every square inch of your garden. It's perfectly acceptable and workable for you to come up with a thumbnail sketch that portrays what your new garden will have by way of features and then elsewhere make a note where necessary of the size of each of these features. So for example, your thumbnail drawing might include a new or existing patio area. Elsewhere, let's say in your notebook, you can include more specific details of this patio: measurements, stone colour, quantities, etc.

The most important thing with any garden design project is that you get started. Don't worry about getting it right or working on creating impressive drawings to show the family and neighbours. Instead get started on your thumbnails and don't worry how childish they might seem.

REFER BACK TO YOUR GARDEN SURVEY

Your Garden Survey information should include:

1. The features that you will be keeping in your garden.
2. Those features that you will be removing from your new garden.
3. Any features that will have to remain in your new garden but will need to be disguised or made less prominent.

If you haven't already got this information worked out, take this book with you, wander around your garden and go through the above checklist.

If you have all of this information to hand, it's a good idea to go through your lists again and make sure you're still happy with what you worked out. Good garden design is all about making changes as you go along so don't be intimidated by deciding to get rid of that ugly garage, lean-to or rarely used greenhouse. All you're doing here is working out a few ideas on a piece of paper. In my workshops I encourage everyone to demolish everything in their garden and start over again with a complete blank canvas.

The trick with thumbnail sketching is to make notes of your ideas either on the same sheets as your drawings or in your notebook.

Once you've completed a rough and as much in-perspective sketch of your garden as you can, you're now ready to pencil in all those features that will remain and those that need to be disguised.

Next include all those features that you want to have in your new garden that you don't already have. For example, additional seating areas.

If you're planning on creating additional planting areas, sketch in where the new areas are going to be.

Once you've finished playing around with your thumbnail sketches, you're ready to create a final drawing. Do this in the same way as you created your Survey Drawing. Only this time, as opposed to having a drawing of what your garden looks like at the moment, you'll have one of what your new garden is going to look like.

So how does it all look?

Once you've completed your drawing, sit back and have a look at it. Take your time here. Personally I like to leave my drawings for a few days or more before returning to them.

What do you think? Does what you're proposing motivate you to undertake the work needed to create the garden, or do you feel it all looks a bit flat and uninspiring? If you think it looks wonderful and fulfils both your practical and inspirational requirements, then great. You're ready to move on and work through the rest of the book, which includes lots of information on how to create your new garden.

I might be wrong here, but I suspect that the drawing you're now looking at is somewhat uninspiring and unimaginative. If this is the case then don't despair, as the rest of this chapter is going to look at ways you can create a really superb design.

THE DESIGN PROCESS EXPLAINED

Designing a garden is nothing more than a sequence of events, as opposed to some sudden inspirational burst of creativity.

Every time I've been asked to design either a new garden for a new house that has nothing but a perimeter fence, or makeover an existing garden, I'm never entirely happy with my initial ideas. Occasionally it might be that a particular design leaps out at me when I first visit the garden that I'm about to redesign, but this is rare. Most of the time I have to go away and do the homework, so to speak. So that's what you're now going to have to do. Get stuck into doing the homework needed to create a truly superb design or redesign. I promise you it's not difficult and you'll have a lot of fun along the way. The system I'm going to show you is the same method I have successfully used year after year.

◆ TIP ◆

The system works because instead of simply trying to come up with design ideas, you follow a thought-provoking, idea-generating process. A sort of brainstorming for gardening!

STEP 1 – REVISIT YOUR GARDEN SURVEY AND NEEDS QUESTIONNAIRE

The first, and I believe the most important, step in the design process is the information you originally gathered when completing your Needs Questionnaire.

Somewhere within those pages of notes are all the answers you need to unlock your creativity. Therefore I want you now to get out your Needs Questionnare. If you haven't already done it, I recommend you waste no more time, grab a pencil and complete it now. It really is that important!

The results of your Needs Questionnaire

The questionnaire concentrates on the three following areas:

1. What do you want from your garden in terms of your sensual and practical needs?
2. What does everyone else living in your household want from the garden?
3. What inspires you in a garden?

Sensual and practical needs

First look to satisfy your sensual needs. After all, gardens are somewhere to be enjoyed!

I invite you to write down all those thing that you'd like from your new garden. Be adventurous here. If your life is full of stressful commuting and you want your garden to be an oasis of calm as far away as possible from work and stress, then ask yourself what sort of features would make it so.

Your list could include all sorts of things, for example the gentle, soothing sound of running water, a hammock in a shady area to relax and read, an area of lawn where you can practise your golf putting, a hot tub to soak away the stress, or a log cabin where you can rediscover your romantic side.

Remember to refer to the five senses for inspiration: what you hear, what you see, what you smell, what you touch and what you taste that really lifts your mood or calms you down. For example, grasses rustling in the fading evening light while you sit on a swinging seat listening to water falling gently somewhere in the distance and the scent of your favourite flower floating on the breeze.

Whatever combination of effects you need to create your perfect mood, you should include them somewhere in your garden. Even if it's only a sheltered place to put a scented outdoor candle, it's better than nothing.

But to have any chance of success your design must also address your practical needs. By practical needs I mean all those features that you need and that will generally stay outside in your garden as opposed to inside your home, for example, a place for your clothes line, tool shed, bike shed and somewhere to winter store your garden furniture, pots, etc.

Meeting the needs of the rest of your household

It is very important at this stage in your planning that you take into account the needs of everyone, including children and any pets you have.

I've worked on gardens in the past where the clients have completely ignored the fact that they have either young children or boisterous dogs when coming up with a new garden design. Wherever possible I try to warn homeowners of the disadvantages of creating garden designs that rely on either delicate and intricate planting schemes or fiddly areas of shingle, because to a child or a dog these features are just crying out to be abused.

For example, when deciding on a suitable surface for our courtyard garden, what I really wanted to do was lay paving stones. However, as we have two relatively large dogs who like to spend time in the garden, we decided to shingle over the area. The advantage is that if the dogs have something unpleasant like a sick tummy, we can simply let them out there and once they've done their business the whole area can be easily hosed down. The dogs also like the shingle, which they pull back into little heaps, which they then lie on. All we have to do to restore the courtyard to its original neat and tidy appearance is run a rake over it.

However, beware of potential conflict between householders' differing needs and tastes!

Were you to have a similar garden to us but as well as having pets you have small children, shingle would be a poor choice as curious children may well start swallowing the small stones. So what might suit some members of your household's needs might not necessarily suit everyone.

On rare occasions, I've seen the altogether unpleasant and I believe unnecessary situation where certain members of households, usually pets, are got rid of because they don't fit in with the new garden design. While I can understand someone's frustration at having bought an expensive specimen tree that the family dog decides to chew and kill, what is clear is that the situation could have been avoided had the householder questioned the suitability of such a purchase.

You should be especially aware of your children's needs. Even if you don't have children at the moment, give some thought to how your household might be looking a few years from now. Or if you're perhaps not planning to stay in your home for very long, remember that when it comes to selling your home potential purchasers may well have children and it's therefore important that you create a child-friendly garden even though you don't want or won't be having children.

For example, the garden should be as much an exciting, safe playground as you can make it. Keep it simple so that children have as large an area as possible to play with their toys.

During warm periods, remember if you've got an inflatable children's paddling pool and you erect it on a lawn that it will, if left more than a day or so, kill the grass underneath. While no real damage will be done, as your lawn will recover, it might be an idea while you're at the planning stage to think about creating a separate area especially for things like inflatable pools, Wendy houses and so on.

If you're going to include a herb and/or vegetable garden, make sure you provide adequate provision for keeping it safe from small children and pets. For example, when we had our large herb garden our dog loved eating his way through all sorts of things. And if he wasn't eating, pulling or lying on top of plants, he was spraying them. So we had to throw away a whole season's otherwise edible crop and redesign the herb garden to include discreet fencing, which kept the dogs out without making the garden look like an allotment.

Children and garden ponds don't go well together. In 2004 fourteen children lost their lives in garden ponds. As I said earlier, I'm called upon more often to remove garden ponds than to create them. So I'd urge you to think carefully before committing yourself to a pond. While undoubtedly a well-designed water feature offers a refreshing and inspirational addition to any garden, it doesn't have to be based on digging a great, deep hole. There are so many successful water feature alternatives to the traditional pond that it's now possible to add a water feature without any of the hassles and dangers associated with a pond.

Don't forget your visitors. If you have elderly relatives who are going to visit you regularly, you should make sure that the area where you situate your seating area is easy to get to and doesn't involve climbing lots of steps or abseiling over rockeries. And if you're planning to create the ultimate summer party garden, remember to create your main seating areas as close to the house as possible, thus allowing for easy access to indoor food preparation, refreshment refrigeration and toilets.

Consider also your long-term gardening plans

Returning once more to your completed Lifestyle Questionnaire, it's now time to consider your long-term gardening plans. How much time will you have available in the future for maintaining your new garden? In my experience there are two great dangers when it comes to gardening projects:

1. Overestimating how much time is available for gardening when everything else has been attended to.
2. Underestimating the amount of time it takes successfully to complete a gardening project.

Since giving up on our large garden and moving to our new home with its courtyard garden, I have had no fewer than four allotment gardens. So desperate have I been to rekindle my love of growing my own herbs and vegetables that I have signed up on four separate occasions for four different allotment plots. The furthest I've ever got with any of the plots has been to dig over one plot and build wooden raised planters on another, and grow a crop of weeds on all the plots. In doing so I have managed to infuriate my allotment neighbours, who worried that my stinging nettles would take over their own neatly laid-out plots, which at the time were thriving vegetable-growing plots.

I still have the letter from the Town Council instructing me to attend to the clearance of my plot or face a fine. As the owner of a garden maintenance company I was embarrassed to say the least by that particular communication and once I got the plot completely cleared of weeds, I gave it back to them.

Time is something that few of us have in great quantities and I strongly recommend you design a garden that won't end up with you being overstressed because you haven't got the time to maintain it. So often I get calls from frustrated gardeners who want me to look after a garden that they lovingly created, only to find that they now lack the time, energy or enthusiasm required to keep it all going.

While I'm not suggesting you simply do as so many do and create the perfect 'low-maintenance' solution by concreting and shingling over your land, I do think that you should be aware that the average-sized garden requires at least three hours every week to keep it looking tidy and under control. By average, I mean a garden that hasn't got much more than a lawn area, flower borders and a few pots here and there.

If you don't enjoy gardening, consider creating a garden with lots of dense shrubbery and lawn. The benefit of this is that you won't have huge areas to weed and you can easily employ a gardener to cut your lawns and hedges on a regular basis if you cannot or don't want to undertake the work yourself. You'll also benefit from a nice, green garden in which the dense shrubs absorb any unwanted outside noises, while the lawn multifunctions as a children's play area and somewhere for the family to sit and relax during the summer, while giving all-year-round colour during those often bleak winter months.

You will have to consider all three of the Lifestyle Questionnaire sections outlined above when deciding on the design of your new garden. My advice is that you start off with a relatively simple, straightforward design and then work from there. At this stage don't get too caught up with trying to create or re-create some complicated structural design you might have either seen or that has come into your head. By starting with a simple design you can use this as the basis either for further expansion and elaboration at a later date, or you can simply keep working on your new garden as time allows and develop it into something more exciting and brilliant.

Most of my successful garden designs have come about on the basis of my client saying all they want is 'a nice simple garden where we can enjoy life and be inspired'.

The problem with grandiose designs is that they are very much a case of all or nothing. Get it right and you'll feel great, but get it wrong and you'll have wasted time, energy, enthusiasm and, most worryingly, money.

So think about all the aspects of your future design and refer back to your completed Lifestyle Questionnaire. Be honest with yourself. If you haven't got much time available now to work in your garden but would like to spend more time gardening, then work out ways of making more time available before committing yourself to a garden design that will only work if you have lots of spare time.

COLOUR IN YOUR GARDEN

Successful garden designs are not just about clever ways of using space but also about creating harmonious colour arrangements. So you'll need to start becoming more 'colour aware' and appreciating the impact a certain colour can have on your garden. For example, if you have a relatively small garden and have red as the dominant colour, the effect will be to create a particularly 'hot' environment, as well as making the garden appear smaller than it is.

Just as red is a hot colour, pastel blues and greens have a cooling effect. Therefore if space is a problem in your garden and you want to create a feeling of airiness and calm, you could use shades of green and blue as your dominant colours, while using red sparingly to create contrast.

Which colours work well and where?

Unfortunately, there is no textbook formula that says such-and-such a colour equates to such-and-such an effect. The only real way of learning how colour and contrast work is to get out in the fresh air and walk around your own neighbourhood and or get out into the countryside. Wherever you choose to go, be on the lookout for colour schemes that work. Look at other people's gardens and see for yourself what the impact of certain colours is. The advantage of seeing other people's gardens is that often you get to see a row of similar houses with more or less the same-size gardens. As you walk past you will see immediately which of those gardens look big and which look much smaller. Stand on the opposite pavement to the properties (discreetly of course!) and look for the colour details in each garden. Ask yourself why some gardens appear smaller?

Generally speaking you'll see that it comes down to either an over-sized central feature, or the illusion is caused by a certain colour scheme. Gardens with green lawns will usually appear larger than those gardens whose owners have either concreted or shingled over any trace of lawn. You'll notice the impact of green not only as a cooling colour, but also as a natural way of creating space.

'Field trips' like these are an important way of getting to appreciate colours and their impact. This is the sort of information you can only gather when out and about or looking at pictures of gardens on television programmes or in glossy magazine features.

Record your findings

Get used to taking your notebook with you wherever you go. Whenever you come across a colour scheme that you think would work well in your own garden, jot down the main colours and if possible draw a thumbnail sketch of how the garden is constructed in terms of hard and soft features. Don't be afraid also to knock on someone's door and ask them for the names of any plants or shrubs that particularly interest you. In my experience other gardeners are generally only too delighted and even flattered to be asked and to help. To date, no one has ever turned me down when I've asked them what such-and-such is and most gardeners usually offer me either a cutting or some seed to take away.

From now on start visiting as many nurseries and public gardens as you can. Nurseries and garden centres are sales-orientated businesses and the successful ones will arrange their shrubs, plants and produce attractively, paying close attention to creating harmonious and complementary colour schemes. Similar to interior design catalogues or paint company brochures, the arrangements have been painstakingly worked out to create the maximum 'buy-me-now' effect. You can benefit from their research and years of trial and error by simply replicating their colour and planting schemes. Don't think that by doing this you are somehow limiting your own creativity or cheating by using someone else's design. You're not. You're simply using a colour scheme and arrangement that has been proven to work, which is far more important than wasting time, money and effort in trying to figure out what works and what doesn't. And of course there's nothing to stop you putting your own creative slant on an existing successful colour scheme.

EXERCISE – FIELD TRIPS

When making field trips or looking around private and public gardens, pay particular attention to the following:

■ The way plants and shrubs are arranged. For example, when you see a border or arrangement that looks attractive, study the way it's put together. What structure has been used to create the effect that you find interesting?

■ Where are the tall shrubs in relation to the smaller ones? Where are the flowers with colour in relation to those that aren't in flower?

■ Study the shape and density of the planted border areas. Are they predominantly straight and narrow or waltzing and deep? Or a combination of both?

- If there is a lawn area, how big is it in relation to the rest of the planting?
- When you see a really attractive garden, ask yourself what is it that makes this garden better than the others you've seen.
- If you're planning to have a garden pond in your garden make sure you keep an eye out for gardens that have ponds. When you find them study closely the structure and size of the pond in relation to the rest of the garden.

Once you've completed your research, make sure you go back over your notes. If in the future you're stuck for ideas, always refer back to your Garden Journal and any pictures you might have taken during your field visits.

STEP 2 – DECIDING ON A STYLE FOR YOUR GARDEN

Once you've decided on what you want from your garden and how much time you will have available to maintain it, it's time for you to decide what style it will take.

While there are lots of styles and themes to choose from, essentially most gardens will be either formal or informal.

FORMAL STYLE

As the name suggests, a formal garden gives the visitor an impression of order, with mostly straight lines and geometric shapes. Many stately homes have formal gardens that lead you up a long, perhaps tree-lined, driveway. The effect is one of suit and tie as opposed to sweatshirt and jeans.

Formal gardens tend to mirror a home's lines and appearance and there is usually some central focal point from which everything else takes it lead, for example a perfectly trimmed yew hedge or a central ornate pond, statue or flowerbed.

An obvious advantage of choosing a formal style for your garden is that it is less difficult to design and consists mostly of straight lines.

When it comes to planting schemes, these again will fall into the overall rigid design, and instead of carefree borders there will be long lines of carefully planted shrubs and flowers, which again create an ordered, structured approach.

The origins of the formal garden

The formal garden design can be traced to Italy during the Renaissance. At the time geometry for both physical structures and planting arrangements became very fashionable.

Features of the Italian formal garden include:

- Vast terraced areas.
- Hard features such as gravel, balustrading and ornamental fountains.
- Herb gardens surrounded by neat, symmetrical lines of box.
- Olive and citrus trees, with pencil-thin cypresses standing guard at the corners.

You don't have to have a large garden to re-create a formal garden. A patio planted with some stone balustrading with aromatic and culinary herbs in terracotta pots and, if space allows, some neatly clipped box is an excellent way of creating an interesting yet extremely simple formal garden.

Obviously if space allows you can create a more extensive garden. You could also consider creating a formal garden in one area of your garden, for example the front garden, and then create an altogether different style for the back garden.

INFORMAL STYLE

With an informal garden there is no rigid design to stick to and here you can be as creative as you like. The obvious advantage of working on an informal design is that it's far easier to create those all-important three winning design elements: tension, mystery and surprise. Gone are the long and often narrow pathways that take the eye to a distant feature. These are replaced instead by sweeping curves where one wonders what is around the next corner. No longer are shrubs and plants kept in neat lines, but instead they are allowed to grow where they are most happy and their foliage can spill beautifully over edges and borders and onto pathways.

The informal garden is generally a hive of activity, where every area takes on a special meaning. The sombre formality of traditional straight-line gardening gives way to a livelier feel, where the garden looks less contrived and more at one with nature. Informal garden designs work particularly well when areas of the garden look out over countryside or coastal landscapes. This allows the designer to create a garden that flows, following the already established curves and intricacies of the existing landscape.

Urban and small gardens also benefit from informality, where instead of long narrow pathways, squared lawns and patio areas, they can meander and flow, losing their 'building plot' appearance and becoming far more inviting spaces.

A potential disadvantage of designing an informal garden is that it is more difficult than designing a formal garden. However, don't let this put you off. My own view is that unless you have a period property that simply cries out for formality, you should indulge your creativity and design your new garden to be as natural as possible.

I believe that your future time spent relaxing and pottering in your new garden will be far more enjoyable if you cannot see the tell-tale signs of rigid formality. So much of our lives today are spent following rules and mission statements and waiting endlessly on phones that it's important for us not to import these frustrations into our gardens. With this in mind, I hope you consider choosing an informal style and allowing your garden to flow more naturally.

OTHER STYLES

There are many other examples of informal styles that you could take inspiration from. For example, there are the classical and traditional styles based on early Greek and Roman architecture, and traditional gardens based on particular historical periods. However, to explore these designs in any great detail would be beyond the scope of this book's brief and I'd suggest that if you're really interested in re-creating a period or classical garden that you have a look at some of the excellent gardening history books that are already available.

COTTAGE GARDENS

At one time the cottage garden enjoyed enormous popularity. With an abundance of flowers and vegetables it really was both a beautiful and functional garden. The theory behind the cottage garden was that the flowers attracted the beneficial insects, which would then feed on the undesirable insects and pests, thus stopping them from causing widespread damage to the vegetables and herbs. Whether or not this actually happened is the subject of much debate among gardeners. However, the cottage garden is enormously pleasing to look at and has a nostalgic chocolate box image that many of us crave after.

A potential drawback of the cottage garden is that it can be incredibly labour intensive, requiring continual dead-heading and watering during the growing season, and can look somewhat depressing during the autumn and winter seasons when nothing flowers. The traditional end-of-season clearance and cutting back of foliage will not suit everyone in terms of the time it takes to complete.

However, if you've got the time and you really do enjoy pottering around your garden, then you should consider a cottage garden style. Even if you don't want to go the full mileage and devote your entire plot to a cottage garden, you could instead set aside a specific area, for example in the front garden, to create a cottage garden planting scheme. This way you can benefit from a colourful display during the summer months while other areas of your garden can be designed and planted to create all-year-round interest.

Cottage gardens really are delightful and will include:

■ Planting schemes comprising a wild arrangement of bright and cheery shrubs, plants and flowers, such as sweet peas, asters, campanula, delphiniums, dianthus, phlox and even runner beans.
■ The ever-popular climbing roses on either stone walls or as neatly kept evergreen hedges to create the ideal borders.

■ A variety of flowers, herbs and vegetables, and if possible some fruit-growing shrubs and trees.

Although on the face of it a cottage garden might seem very informal in its appearance, its structure is anything but. To be successful, a cottage garden needs to follow a clear, predefined structure. Boundaries are usually straight edged with neatly trimmed hedges, and the planting areas and beds are divided into separate, easy-to-work sections. Very much like a professional florist works to a clear design plan, a cottage garden also works to a similar template. As soon as a cottage garden bursts into bloom it loses any appearance of formality as flowers, shrubs and plants spill and fall over pathways and grow up, down, across and under each other, giving everywhere a beautiful natural feel.

Over time a cottage garden starts to self-seed, with an ever-greater variety and abundance of flowers. So the benefit of a cottage garden is that it continues to grow more beautiful and magical as time goes on.

CONTEMPORARY GARDEN STYLE

The essence of contemporary garden style is when the garden design complements a modern house. A contemporary garden tends to rely more on materials and objects for effect than on abundant planting schemes or soft features.

If you've a busy lifestyle and won't be getting much gardening time and you like the idea of a modern, minimalist garden, you should consider creating a contemporary garden.

For inspiration, browse through the many interior design magazines and those magazines featuring interiors and gardens, as well as staying on the lookout for ideas and inspiration from the area where you live.

Water, wood and metal tend to feature in modern gardens, where decking areas are created around or over water with some form of metal or even wooden structure as the focal point.

You could also base your new garden on a recycled theme and choose only those hard features that have been manufactured using recycled materials. For example, instead of using excavated shingle and stone, you could opt for the altogether more environmentally friendly alternative of recycled glass chippings. A number of suppliers are now taking glass and recycling it into minute decorative garden chippings which can be used in much the same way as stone chippings. The system for recycling has been so well developed now that there is no risk of being cut or injured and the overall appearance is far more spectacular and interesting.

A contemporary garden design can be an ideal approach for a small garden that surrounds a modern property. The minimalist garden really does work well when space is at a premium, and if you're not keen on spending hours maintaining your garden then this is an ideal and obvious solution.

JAPANESE-STYLE GARDEN

With our busy lifestyles, it's not surprising that Japanese-style gardens have become increasingly popular. The Japanese garden is predominantly low maintenance once constructed. However, constructing a Japanese-style garden if anything requires very careful planning and a fairly generous budget, as much of the construction will require stone, statues and other features.

There are three main styles of Japanese garden:

- Shin – A formal garden.
- Gyo – A semi-formal garden.
- So – An informal garden.

The Shin formal garden will be familiar to many with its brightly painted wooden bridges and stone lanterns. Navigation will be via smooth paving and it will have a water feature.

The semi-formal Gyo garden won't have the brightly painted wooden bridges, but instead will have simple stone bridges. The smooth paving will be replaced with assorted paving slabs, and aged statues will be placed around the garden.

The So informal garden will be like our gardens in that it will reflect nature more by using natural materials and planting.

Each design will have water features. Whether this be a bamboo deer scarer (you can buy these ready-made in garden centres) or a stream or granite water basin is up to you. But water is a main part of the design. A stream is symbolic of one's passage through life.

Rocks are used in Japanese gardens to replicate landscape. Where used, rocks should resemble the shapes of mountains.

Sand and gravel are used to represent clouds or water, which is why in a real Japanese garden the stone and sand is frequently raked. Most replica Japanese gardens substitute white chippings instead of using the sand that would be used in an authentic garden.

WATER GARDENS

Depending on your interests, you may wish to create a water garden in your main garden area. I've seen long, narrow plots transformed into one great long rectangular black-water pond, which then becomes the centre-piece of the garden. The pond is either surrounded by wooden decking or ornamental stone and the ponds walls are often raised above the ground level of the garden so that you can sit on top of them.

As I previously said, with this design approach you'd want to be fairly confident that a water garden was exactly what you wanted and that you intended to stay in your property for the foreseeable future. It's a fact that many homeowners want either a lake or a pond as the central feature of their garden. In my time gardening I have only ever come across one client who wanted their garden turned into a lake, which they eventually did using a different contractor. When I later visited a neighbouring property, I took the opportunity of looking at the finished garden from a back bed-room window. What struck me about the whole thing was how out of place it all looked in a modern home. My own view is that this sort of garden is more suitable as a central feature for a hotel or office building as opposed to a small, domestic garden. However, if that's what you want in your garden – go for it!

MEDITERRANEAN GARDENS

A number of years ago, Mediterranean garden styles became very popular. Much of this interest was created by the abundance of garden makeover television programmes, which regularly featured Mediterranean themes. Like everything that follows a trend, there are good and bad examples, and some people seemed to believe that all that was necessary to create a Mediterranean garden was to paint a fence blue or purple!

Mediterranean countries generally use a lot of hard materials such as stones and gravel in their gardens. And the choice of colour and texture of these stones is mirrored through the property and garden. Deep blues and burnt orange with terracotta pots and paving inspire a beautifully warm, Mediterranean atmosphere, but to be successful the colour theme needs to flow and be visible not just in the garden but also on the property. This can be achieved by either repainting the outside of your property with a Mediterranean theme or simply painting certain parts of it, for example the windows or ledges, or even adding brightly painted window shutters.

Start thinking about how you could create natural shady areas. An often overlooked feature of the Mediterranean garden is the beautiful big parasols used on patios. Or you could build beams over your patio and seating areas, to provide shade as well as a suitable climbing frame for plants and shrubs.

If like me your garden is a simple a courtyard, then providing you have a suitable climate it could lend itself to the Mediterranean garden style. Small details such as choosing a variety of terracotta pots of all shapes and sizes and painting boundary walls in white with doors in brilliant deep blues and yellows are all simple ways of creating a Mediterranean atmosphere. Incidentally, the reason that walls are painted white in the Med is to reflect the light away and thus keep the interior of any buildings cool. The benefit of using white on your walls is that it creates an excellent backcloth for any striking Mediterranean shrubs and trees you might have.

Even if space is a problem and all you have is a courtyard area, try at least to have one tall specimen shrub such as a palm tree. The importance of selecting taller shrubs is that they are ideal for casting shade. Make sure also to include some evergreens in your planting scheme, for example junipers and cypresses. If space allows you could also include a phormium. In every garden I have had, I have had a phormium. Their striking architectural shape adds interest and intrigue to even the most sedate site. The downside is that they do grow and eventually dwarf their setting. However, my view has always been that when they get too large for the garden, I simply dig them up and start again.

Popular plants and shrubs for a Mediterranean garden will include: palms, phormiums, yuccas and cordylines, while ivy makes for an excellent drought-resistant climber for overhead frames or pergolas. For fragrances you can include French lavenders, artemisia, and jasmine is a truly authentic Mediterranean climber.

STEP 3 – FINALISE WHAT YOU WANT TO INCLUDE IN YOUR DESIGN

As you can see, designing your garden involves making decisions and following a process until you come to a conclusion. The final step in creating your new garden plan is to combine all your needs and those of the people living with you and put them all together in one plan.

Don't worry too much about where you're going to position everything. Later I'll give you some suggestions and advice on the best places to position features such as patios, seating areas, ponds, etc. For the moment, just concentrate on what's going into your new garden and what style of garden you'd like to have. You may of course want to have a mixture of garden styles, for example a formal front garden that will be kept neat and tidy and an informal back garden where the children and pets can enjoy a safe, fun environment.

Take your time when making your decisions. Discuss them all with everyone in your household who will be affected. When you've got all angles covered and listened to everyone's views, add the final details to the plan.

In the next chapter, I'll show you what's involved in creating a Planting Plan for your new garden. It may of course be that you don't need to make any alterations or additions to your existing planting arrangements and are simply constructing your new garden around them.

◆ CHECKLIST ◆

- ◆ For the purposes of planning your first garden, you should only really concentrate on creating a Functional Plan.

- ◆ Thumbnail sketching is a great way of designing your garden without worrying too much about making mistakes. Make lots of thumbnail sketches showing a variety of potential layouts.

- ◆ Designing your garden is a process as opposed to relying on your inspiration.

- ◆ It is time now to choose a style for your garden. If space allows, you can include a number of styles for different areas.

- ◆ You should now have decided on what your practical needs are and how you can meet those needs in your new garden.

6

CREATING AND WORKING WITH PLANTING PLANS

DON'T BE PUT OFF BY LACK OF KNOWLEDGE

If you're not an experienced gardener and don't really know one plant from the other, then don't let this put you off. All you're doing at this stage is deciding on what areas in your garden you will create for planting and getting a rough idea of what form, shape and size that planting will take. Even lifetime gardeners struggle to identify every plant and shrub. It is far more important that you start working on planting schemes at this early stage, as opposed to realising at some point in the future that your new garden doesn't really work because you've failed to address planting in your design.

CHOOSING PLANTING AREAS

If you've just purchased a new home from a property developer, the chances are your garden is going to be what the sales staff euphemistically refer to as a 'blank canvas'. They will tell you that the great thing about having a garden with nothing in it is that you get the opportunity to release your creative side. Whether this is the case or not is doubtful, as most new-build gardens I've worked in have had enormous problems to overcome before any creative juices could flow. Problems such as buried rubble, which has included plastic, building materials and all sorts of contamination. In one garden I even uncovered a tarmac road underneath eight inches of topsoil that the developer had spread over the site in a last effort to create the perfect 'blank canvas.'

However, once you get to work preparing and clearing your site (which I'll show you how to do in the next chapter), you're then ready to dress the garden with plants, shrubs and trees. An obvious advantage of the new home garden is that you're free to construct borders without having to revise existing schemes. A potential drawback is that you're first going to have to work out the various crucial points in your garden – i.e. where are the sunniest spots, the shady areas, the exposed areas, the damp areas etc., – before deciding on what to include and where to position it.

The other scenario is revising an existing garden with already defined planting areas. For example, borders running the length of your garden or alongside paths and patio areas, and mature trees, shrubs or hedges may be already in place. Here the novice gardener has the advantage of being able to see what is successfully growing in their garden and where the particular shrubs and plants are most happy. When it comes to planting, you must remember that your needs in terms of where you'd like such-and-such a shrub to grow come a poor second to the shrub's needs. Every gardener I know has learnt this lesson the hard way. All of us at some time have either moved a mature shrub or plant to somewhere else in the garden where we feel it would be better suited, only to find the shrub withers and dies or limps on in obvious distress.

When creating a Planting Plan there are a number of factors you are going to have to consider:

1. How the Planting Plan could help solve or alleviate any local environmental problems.
2. How the Planting Plan will fit in with the style of garden that you're proposing.
3. Whether to increase or reduce the size of any existing planting areas.
4. How you can use planting to create a more private garden. For example dense and taller planting around your boundaries can reduce what others see and hear in your garden. Or a strategically placed tree can create more privacy by blocking out someone else's view of your garden.

5. What existing plants or shrubs need to be moved or removed.
6. Whether or not planting areas will be focal points of the garden or creat background colour and interest.
7. Potential cost of planting a new garden.

PLANTING TO SOLVE ENVIRONMENTAL PROBLEMS

You'll recall from an earlier chapter how important it is to walk around your existing garden and note down your likes and dislikes, particularly in relation to outside features such as traffic noise, pollution, smells, etc. The first priority of any Planting Plan should be to address these things.

I have visited countless gardens where the owners have complained about the impact of traffic noise on the enjoyment of their gardens. Without exception all these gardens have one thing in common – a lack of mature and dense shrubbery. Garden boundaries have consisted of wafer-thin larch lap fencing, sporadic planting of the occasional evergreen, or nothing at all. Unsurprisingly, the garden and home suffer from an unacceptable level of traffic noise. The obvious solution is to create a dense, evergreen hedge bordering the entire garden.

Other environmental pollutants can include noisy neighbours. Here again, a dense, mature Planting Plan can be introduced to reduce the noise levels and improve privacy.

♦ TIP ♦

A good Planting Plan can reduce or even eliminate unwanted environmental noise and odour pollution.

So your first priority when working on your Planting Plan is to address all your environmental dislikes.

PLANTING TO SUIT THE STYLE OF YOUR NEW GARDEN

Plants can be chosen on the basis of their:

1. Size.
2. Colour.
3. Shape.
4. Texture.
5. Smell.
6. Sound. For example, tress or grasses rustling in the wind.
7. Taste. For example, edible crops, culinary herbs.
8. Healing ability. For example, medicinal herbs.

As you can see, plants can satisfy all our sensual needs. Their contribution to the success of your new garden should never be underestimated.

The plants you choose will have enormous impact on your new garden in terms of shape, colour and size. Hence, if you want to create a formal style, you'll need plants that can be easily maintained in a formal atmosphere. For example, yew is an excellent shrub to include as a formal hedging and can be easily shaped. One client of mine has a spectacular topiary yew hedge running the width of her rear garden in front of her swimming pool. The hedge is shaped similar to a castle wall complete with turrets, towers and battlement positions. Neatly clipped box hedging surrounding the planting beds completes the formal structure.

I also have clients whose garden is entirely informal, and their planting scheme reflects this style exactly. Instead of long, neat hedges they have meandering borders that are home to a variety of shrubs and plants that spill and tumble everywhere. Weeping willows create excellent privacy screens without taking away from the natural, ad-hoc feeling. Shrubs, roses and a variety of perennials blend in wonderfully with the informal property that they surround.

When creating your Planting Plan, you'll constantly need to cross-reference your choices with your chosen styles. While some plants and shrubs will be ideal in either a formal or informal arrangement, others, for example box and yew, don't blend in well with informality. They have a certain austerity and order about them that will not suit every garden.

INCREASING OR REDUCING EXISTING PLANTED AREAS

If one of your priorities is to create a low-maintenance garden, you're going to have to evaluate your garden's present planting arrangement in relation to your future needs. Generally, larger and more mature plants and shrubs need less ongoing maintenance than a herbaceous border. Herbaceous borders grow, thrive and flower all in one season and then die back during the dormant (winter) season. Herbaceous borders are a feature of cottage gardens, and if you are planning a cottage garden you will need to allow plenty of growing space for your herbaceous delights.

Alternatively, if you are planning to create a contemporary garden where planting will take on a more minimalist approach, you might need to reduce the size of your existing borders or do away with them altogether. There is no rule that says your borders must run alongside each and every perimeter wall, yet how many gardeners stop at nothing to ensure their neat, narrow borders run like hard shoulders against their straight, monotonous pathways? Soulless, unimaginative and thoroughly avoidable.

So now is the time to decide on border sizes. Too big, and you will need to look at ways of reducing them, which will in turn impact on other soft and hard features. For example, if you already have a concrete or otherwise permanent footway running alongside the border, you all need to work out what you are going to do with it when the border is reduced. Likewise, if you want to increase the size of the border, you're going to have to remove all or part of the existing footway.

I've come across situations where my clients have gone out and purchased expensive, mature shrubs and then found that the border where they wanted to plant them is too small and because of the positioning of a concrete footway it has been impossible to extend it.

Remember that when it comes to choosing plants, you should allow for future growth and spread. Not only will most plants and shrubs grow taller over time, but they will also grow wider.

WHICH PLANTS NEED TO BE MOVED OR REMOVED

An easy way of transforming an existing garden is simply to remove a large and unwanted planting feature. For example, I had a client who complained that their seated patio area was too small for their needs. When I measured the existing floor area, it was actually relatively large. The problem wasn't so much a lack of patio space but the enormous phormium that overshadowed the patio area, thus reducing its size and the amount of light. My suggestion to my clients was to remove the phormium and create a new planting scheme around the existing patio. The results were instant and spectacular.

When planning your first garden, don't be afraid of removing large planting features if they don't meet your future requirements. I've seen clients move into new homes and keep toiling away at a rose garden they neither wanted nor had any great interest in simply on the basis that the rose garden was always there and the garden would suffer if it were gone. The reality is that your garden won't suffer at all provided you create something either to take the removed feature's place or take the focus of attention away from where the feature once was.

Be bold and brave!

CHOOSING PLANTING AS FOCAL POINT OR BACKGROUND EFFECT

Following on from what I said in the above examples of the rose garden and the phormium, you will need to decide whether planting will be part of your garden's overall atmosphere or the main focus of attention. For example, the cottage garden relies on plants, shrubs and foliage as the focal point of the garden, while contemporary garden style focuses more on the hard structures of the garden and property and the minimalist planting scheme is secondary.

Even if you're simply going to make over your front garden you should consider if it could be enhanced by including a solitary planting, for example a tree or large shrub, as a focus of attention. The benefit of having a planting

scheme as a focal point is that you can draw the eye away from some existing undesirable feature, for example an uninspiring property frontage.

You don't have to live in a cottage to create a successful, workable cottage garden. One of our previous properties was a relatively unattractive post-war bungalow with a bland concrete driveway. The property was completely transformed by creating a cottage-style garden to the front, side and rear. Visitors to the property couldn't believe that it was the same house. They looked everywhere for signs of alteration, but were surprised to discover that everything was unchanged.

If at the moment your garden lacks any sort of planting focus and you're unhappy with the overall outward appearance of your property, you should consider using plants and foliage as the major focus of attention. This technique is common practice in the interior design business, where faced with lifeless rooms, designers introduce additional features to create interest and intrigue.

On the other hand, if you're thrilled with the architectural appearance of your home, you may wish to use it as the focal point and have planting schemes working discreetly in the background.

A word of caution. You should avoid the all-too-common mistake of creating a large, often circular, bed, which gets filled annually with an unimaginative arrangement of seasonal bedding plants, giving the overall effect of a local authority park.

POTENTIAL COSTS OF CREATING ADDITIONAL PLANTING

Whenever I watch a garden makeover programme, I try to calculate how much is being spent, including any additional planting. Invariably the costs are enormous and I believe so great that they are out of reach of most people's budgets. For example, a common sight is to see the television gardener creating the hard features and framework for the new garden. Once finished, the area is entirely devoid of any plants and shrubs. After the commercial break we rejoin the presenter in a garden centre saying how much he likes such-and-such tree or shrub. We then cut back to the garden site, where a large lorry unloads fully grown trees, shrubs and plants to create the finished garden.

It is entirely unfair of the programme makers to do this, as most people would never be able to afford such elaborate and mature specimens. The majority of us who want to buy a new tree will have to settle for something that is small and spindly and will take a number of years to mature. Which means we might have to wait years for our garden to fully mature before we can fully appreciate how the design works.

I always advise clients that it will take anywhere between three and seven years before they really start to enjoy the benefit of their new garden in terms of planting arrangements.

If money isn't a problem, then fine. Save the waiting, and go out and buy the large specimen trees, shrubs and plants you want. But if your situation is like mine, and you're always watching budgets, be aware how easy it is to spend literally hundreds of pounds at a garden centre and walk away with very little.

The easiest way of reducing potential overspending on planting arrangements is to save as much of your existing planting as you can. Don't be too quick with the axe or spade. Wherever you can, try to retain mature trees and shrubs. Look for ways of keeping shrubs by relocating them if you're not happy with where they are at the moment. Remember to consider the needs of whatever you're moving in terms of water, light, aspect and soil conditions.

FACTORS IN DECIDING ON A FINAL PLANTING PLAN

When deciding on a Planting Plan, you need to look at it from two angles:

1. What the garden will look like immediately after you have completed it.
2. What it will look like at various points in the future, for example after year one, year two, and so on.

Obviously if you're not planning to stay in your present home for long, you should try to choose a planting scheme that's relatively immediate in its results. If you're planning to be around for a long time you can take your time with your Planting Plan and do as many gardeners successfully do, which is to add to it as budgets allow. Instead of socks, nail varnish or CDs for Christmas or birthdays, ask for plants, shrubs and even packets of seeds. It all adds up!

WAYS TO REDUCE THE COSTS OF PLANTING

◆ Check your local paper's small advertisement section for gardeners either selling plants privately, or offering mature shrubs and trees 'free to anyone who'll dig them up and take them away'.
◆ End-of-season clearance sales at garden centres. The last thing a garden centre needs at the end of the season is to be left with lots of stock, so they usually clear unwanted stock at greatly reduced prices.
◆ Avoid the temptation to have an instant garden and instead buy smaller plants and shrubs and patiently bring them on in your garden.
◆ Purchase seeds and grow your own plants and shrubs instead of buying ready-grown planting stock.

FINAL STEPS TO CREATING YOUR PLANTING PLAN

1. Decide on a list of plants and shrubs that would be suitable for your new garden.
2. When planning your list, remember to address your practical needs as well as your inspirational needs.
3. Decide where your new planting and shrubs are going to go and if you require any additional planting areas or to increase the size of your existing borders.

4. Decide on any planting that you might be getting rid of in your new garden. You may not like some existing shrub or plant or you may find that it poses a potential danger to your children. For example, berberis is particularly prickly and you may feel it poses a risk.

5. If you wish, draw up a Planting Plan either by including it in your already completed Functional Plan or by creating a separate Planting Plan.

◆ CHECKLIST ◆

◆ When it comes to planting, don't be put off by any lack of knowledge or worry that you don't know the names of all the shrubs and plants in your garden.

◆ Plan your planting scheme to blend in with the style of your new garden.

◆ Choose plants for what they can do for you in terms of your practical and inspirational needs.

◆ A well-planned planting scheme can reduce unwanted environmental pollution, including noise and odours.

◆ Tall or dense planting schemes can create additional privacy.

◆ Beware of the potential cost of planting on your budget. It's easy to allow these costs to go out of control.

◆ Wherever possible look to save money on your planting budget by being creative in where you source your planting stock.

◆ Draw up your Planting Plan either as part of your Functional Plan or on a separate sheet of paper.

7

ROUGH GUIDE TO POSITIONING ANYTHING

What I'm going to do now is give you a rough guide on positioning common soft and hard features. Remember every garden is different in terms of size, quirks and where in the country you live, so what follows is simply a general guide as opposed to a rigid set of gardening rules.

PLANTS AND SOFT FEATURES

Obviously when it comes to deciding where to plant soft features, including hedges, trees, shrubs, etc., you should be aware of how large they will grow and equally importantly, how fast this will happen. Don't forget, as I previously said, you'll need to ensure that in whatever position you choose for your shrubs and plants they're happy with it too. Sun-loving plants won't last long in a cold, damp area and those that thrive in such conditions won't like to be planted in full sun.

You should also be aware that shrubs *spread*. This is the term given to how wide a shrub will grow, which is important when working out how far you need to plant it from building lines, pathways, etc.

PONDS

The position of your pond is something you cannot afford to get wrong. You'd be amazed at how many ponds I've been asked to maintain and clean that have been built under a tree or a belt of trees. When I've questioned my customers as to why they decided to place their pond under a tree, a common reply is that they thought the fish would benefit from the shade afforded by the tree's canopy. The downside of this is that when the tree sheds its leaves they fall straight into the water, where they cause considerable damage and nuisance. Even when the leaves aren't falling into the water there is lots of other tree-associated debris coming down. For example, rotten branches, bark, etc.

When positioning your pond, try to place it so that it is not going to suffer from contamination from another soft feature. As I said, under trees is an obvious poor choice, but so is in the middle of a lawn where it risks getting sprayed with lawn cuttings every time you cut the grass.

So where should you position your pond? Wherever possible, try to position your pond in full sun as this will encourage water plants to grow, which will in turn improve the quality of your water, making for easier maintenance and helping to promote healthy fish and any wildlife living in your pond.

Every garden is different, but you should ensure your pond has sufficient 'breathing space' around it. This means giving it a nice large area free from interference and also a position where it's not going to get in your way. Personally, I like a pond to be created by a hard-standing area, for example a patio or shingled area, or enclosed by decking. A pond surrounded by decking giving the impression that the water continues underneath is truly magical and inspirational, and breaks up the water feature into something far more interesting.

If your garden is really small, then you could opt for a ready-made raised pond which you can position on your seating area. This means that both you and your pond can enjoy whatever sun is available, with the added bonus that the pond if planted correctly can make a really interesting and attractive feature for your patio.

If you're planning a water feature that won't include plants or fish, for example a pebble pond, then you don't have to be so particular as to where it's positioned. Again, try to avoid positioning it anywhere near or under deciduous trees as when they shed their leaves they will create an unwelcome nuisance in blocking up the stones and filter systems.

STATUES, FIGURES, BIRDBATHS AND BENCHES

All of these are popular features in gardens and, provided they are placed correctly, can add interest and depth. Again the important thing is that they're of the right proportion so as not to look out of place. My personal choice is to position these features in a particular area that is either offset or away from the main garden. For example, you could position a bench in a quiet area of the garden where you can sit and read, soaking up vistas and atmosphere tucked away from the main thoroughfare of the home. Or you could tuck your favourite statue in a border away from immediate view, as another feature for visitors to discover when they walk around the garden. The surprise element creates its own pleasing effect.

VEGETABLE AND HERB GARDENS

If you're planning on including a vegetable and herb garden in your design then you're obviously going to have to position your garden where it fits in with the rest of the plan. Lots of gardeners position their veggie garden at the furthest point from their home as they consider this type of garden to be too unsightly and somewhat unruly to be part of the all-important vista from the window of their lounge or kitchen. Thus the veggie garden gets hidden either as part of a side garden or behind the main garden. Various methods are then used to screen it away. For example, some people choose trellising with a central archway leading into the vegetable garden, while others take advantage of features already in place, such as walls, hedges and fences.

The advantage of tucking the vegetable garden away like this is that the crops themselves benefit from being sheltered not just from the wind and rain but also from domestic pets and children who if left unchecked can destroy literally months of hard work in an instant.

One of the disadvantages of siting your vegetable garden away from the home is that when the weather is bad you have a long way to go to cut a sprig of parsley or dig up some carrots. My favourite way of overcoming this problem is to plant a small culinary herb garden in an area as close to the kitchen as possible. Thus when you're in the kitchen preparing a meal and you need some herbs, all you have to do is pop out the back momentarily and cut them fresh. If you haven't yet tried new potatoes with fresh garden mint, you don't know what you're missing.

If, like me, you have only a courtyard or very small garden with nowhere suitable to create a herb garden you can still grow herbs in pots and containers. If you've pets and you're worried about them urinating on herbs, all you have to do is create a hanging herb garden. You can do this simply by buying or building your own simple wooden shelves which you then hang up either on a wall, fence or even a tree where you can grow your herbs safely out of reach of pets and children. Or you could buy or build some window boxes or troughs which you could use for growing herbs. Then all you have to do is open your window and cut whatever you want.

Herb and vegetable gardens are a great addition to any garden design, and if you haven't already considered including them I'd recommend you create a small area somewhere for growing edible produce. Nothing beats the taste and smells created by your own home-grown herbs. While vegetable growing does require some planning and it can take a bit of time to get used to the seasonal vegetable-growing calendar, herb growing is relatively easy and something that children really do enjoy participating in. I've seen many children who have previously had no interest in gardening become completely hooked when vegetable and herb growing have been introduced. Even adults who cringe at the thought of gardening suddenly become interested when they realise that there's more to it than simply weeding and cutting lawns.

In one home I owned I devoted the entire garden save for a small lawn area to herb and vegetable growing. When unexpectedly we decided to move house, I invited in the usual round of estate agents, some of whom said that in their opinion the herb garden would raise objections among potential purchasers. Perhaps they were right and we unwittingly reduced the number of prospective customers viewing the property, but the house quickly sold to a retired couple who fell in love with the garden and the whole idea of working in it.

I raise this simply to flag up the potential problem of creating a large vegetable garden if you're not planning to stay very long in the property.

SHEDS, GREENHOUSES AND SUMMERHOUSES

Again there are no stringent rules on where you should position any buildings you're planning to include in your new garden. Obviously when it comes to choosing a site for your greenhouse you'll need to position it where it's going to benefit from natural light as opposed to being tucked away in a dark corner. But you also need to make sure that wherever you position it you don't have to trample down potentially wet grass to work in it when the weather's bad. When in the past I've had a greenhouse (I love them because they extend the growing season so much and are great for bringing on herbs), I've positioned it where it benefits from natural light without getting in the way of the main garden area. I've also ensured it has had its own specially created hard-standing area and is still easily accessible from the kitchen. Wherever possible I've kept it away from sitting immediately behind fences or boundary walls for fear of it being damaged by neighbours' children's footballs or anyone throwing anything over the fence from outside. One thing you should be aware of when it comes to greenhouses is that in periods of particularly stormy weather, panes can be blown out and glass will literally spray everywhere, so it's worth keeping it away from lawn areas or where children normally play.

Obviously when it comes to sheds and summerhouses you can position them anywhere. Sheds are generally better off being positioned in otherwise redundant areas or corners as far out of view of the main garden as possible. Garden sheds are useful for storing tools and equipment but can if you're not careful become a dumping ground for all sorts of things, which can mean you have to fight your way in just to get a spade or fork.

Summerhouses are ideally positioned where they give the best view of the garden. Many of my clients have preferred to position their summerhouses as far away from the main home as possible, thus giving them the feeling of complete detachment and allowing them to soak up the atmosphere of their beautiful gardens. Many people I know literally camp out in their summerhouses when the weather allows – a romantic evening away from home without the hassle of motorway travel and expensive accommodation.

HOME GARDEN OFFICES

With an ever-increasing number of people working from home, the office in the garden is becoming a popular alternative to the spare room or makeshift office in the lounge. If you work from home or are considering doing so then it's worth investigating how you could create an office in your garden. A number of companies now offer a specialist service where they will deliver a fully insulated building to your garden. Generally speaking you won't require planning permission but you should check with your local authority to make sure that what you're intending to purchase comes within the permitted planning regulations.

Once your local authority has confirmed that planning permission isn't required, you should contact the company you're intending to purchase from and ask for their advice as to where you should position the building. I say this as there are a number of practical factors that will have to be taken into consideration, including what type of base will have to be constructed to take the office and also things like installing electricity, etc.

You will also want to be sure that when the building arrives it fits into the allocated area. When it comes to measuring structures and creating large enough areas to take them it's all too easy to get it wrong. Even the professionals come unstuck here, so make sure you spend enough time discussing your project with the manufacturers of your home office.

CHILDREN'S PLAY AREAS

The most important thing when considering where to position your children's play area is that you can easily keep an eye on it. Many of my clients have opted to devote the area immediately in front of their kitchen window to a play area, so that while they're working in the kitchen they can watch what's going on outside. Another consideration is proximity to gateways, entrances and the like. Obviously if your garden is completely enclosed you won't have this problem. However, if your garden has a side path without a gate or anything to block it, you'll need as part of your design to prioritise closing off any areas where children could escape unseen out of the main garden and into the road. If your garden is relatively small then you should be able to keep an eye on children wherever they are.

If you have children, now's the time to give some thought to their needs and how these will be catered for in the new garden. As well as considering the actual structures you might like to include for your children, for example sandpits, trampoline areas, playhouses and so on, also think in terms of creating a child-friendly design.

On occasions I've been asked to lay certain areas of shingle by clients who have children. When I've pointed out the potential dangers of adding lots of tiny stones to a garden, many have chosen alternatives. However, those few who haven't have without exception regretted their decision, as tiny hands have enjoyed nothing more than to grab handfuls of this tempting material with its lovely colours and spray it all over daddy and mummy's new lawn.

Decorative bark is another thing you need to be careful with. If you're planning to include it in your new garden you need to ensure that the bark you purchase is suitable for children. Professional landscapers specialising in creating public children's play areas use a specially prepared bark chipping that isn't full of potentially dangerous chemicals or colourings.

A final word on bark and play areas. If you have pet dogs or cats bark can become a favourite area for toileting, with the obvious drawback that you cannot see anything until it's too late. And even if you do it's virtually impossible to either scoop or bag up when stuck to bark. My advice would be that if you have pets and children to avoid bark as a material.

SEATING AREAS

Possibly the most important practical area in your garden! It's here where you sit and enjoy the vistas and smells, soak up the atmosphere and, weather permitting, eat alfresco. Obviously you'll want to choose for your seating area a position where you can enjoy the most sunshine, which depending on your garden may not always be possible. For example, it may be that the sun shines most at the end of your garden and not around the immediate vicinity of your property. By situating your seating area at the far end of the garden, you are potentially inviting all sorts of inconveniences. For example, you'll be further away from your kitchen, which can hamper the preparation and bringing out of food. You also have to trek down the garden every time you want to spend a few quiet moments sitting outside. When guests call you might find you're too far away to hear them ring the door bell. You're also far away from the loo, which for some can represent a big problem.

Ideally you should try to position your seating area where it will get the most sunshine and also be as convenient to your home as possible. When you cannot accommodate both of these factors, you should consider convenience and accessibility first. You could also consider creating two separate seating areas: a main patio area outside your house, with a secondary seating area in the sunniest area. The secondary seating area needn't necessarily be a patio area. You could simply have an arbour or a bench, or even a few hammocks which you could take up and down when needed.

The size of your main seating area will depend on the available space in your garden. However, a common mistake by the first-time garden designer is to underestimate the 12ft × 12ft (3.6m × 3.6m) required to accommodate a relatively small table and four chairs. Indeed, many of the outdoor wooden furniture sets now available in garden centres will require a greater area. And if your patio area is raised above your main garden, you're going to have to make sure that the area is greater still to allow care-free navigation around the table, as opposed to risking falling over the edge of the patio every time someone gets up from the table.

CHAIRS AND GARDEN FURNITURE

While we're on the subject of seating areas, let's talk briefly about the choices available when it comes to seats and tables. When you visit a garden centre or browse an online catalogue you'll see that there's an enormous variety to choose from, ranging from cheap, white plastic sets to relatively expensive bespoke metal designs. Obviously your choice will depend on what budget you have available, so when planning your new garden don't forget to budget for garden furniture.

Personally, I don't favour the plastic sets as they do little to enhance the hard work you've put into creating your new garden. However, if you have to go plastic then don't be tempted to go for something that's plastic but made to look like metal. A few years ago, I was tempted to purchase a plastic garden set, which had been designed to look like metal. Initially it looked okay but as our often inhospitable seaside elements began to take their toll, the colour of the furniture began to fade and crazing appeared intermittently throughout, leaving everyone in no doubt that it was a plastic imitation and a poor one at that.

Round about the same time, relatives purchased a wooden set, which really did look superb. It certainly cost a lot more than what we paid, but whereas our set took away from our garden our relatives' wooden set enhanced theirs and showed off their superb raised patio area. Today, some ten years on, our plastic set is taking up valuable landfill space while the wooden set continues to enhance our relatives' patio and will give many more years of pleasure and beauty.

When it comes to overall finish you don't want anything that looks contrived or staged. Far better to go for a basic, practical, plastic garden furniture set to get you started and then when future budgets allow it to go for something in either wood or metal that complements your new garden and home.

If you are planning to purchase a wooden set, make sure the wood comes from a sustainable forest. It's becoming more common now for furniture manufacturers to declare where their timbers come from. Beware of those that don't. What's good for your garden must also be good for our greater environment.

LAWN AREAS

If your garden is large enough, you should try to include a lawn area. Some of the advantages of having a lawn are:

- It's a natural and safe additional or main area for children to play.
- It's an additional area for you to sit or lie on when the weather allows.
- In hot weather or if your garden has an overreliance on hard features, a lawn is a great way of introducing a natural cooling, refreshing feature into your garden.
- Lawns offer all-year-round colour.
- A good lawn can really enhance the other features in your garden. Colourful borders are brought to life by offering a beautiful green carpet to frame them.
- Your lawn doesn't have to follow a standard square or rectangular shape and can be laid to whatever shape you want. A circular or half-moon lawn breaks up even the dullest of long, narrow gardens.
- Lawns don't have to be laid on the ground. You can have raised lawns growing over sheds, roofs and garages.

I'm a great fan of lawns. Sadly, our courtyard is too small to accommodate a lawn, otherwise I'd have one. The importance of introducing shades of cooling green can never be underestimated. Certainly a shaped lawn as suggested above is a great way of breaking up a long, narrow, uninspiring garden. When considering a lawn, try to get away from the concept that lawns must follow traditional square or rectangular shapes. It's so easy to cut a new shape in an existing lawn using a half-moon cutter, and if you're laying a new lawn with turfs they can easily be cut into whatever shape you want. In a later chapter, I'll show you what's involved in laying a new lawn.

When it comes to positioning, lawns need light. Therefore a full-sun position would be ideal or alternatively somewhere with partial shade. Damp and dark areas aren't great for lawns. If you have a lawn at the moment that is either too boggy in the winter and devoid of any growth in the summer, you'll probably find that it is suffering from a lack of natural light. This is common when a lawn runs the length of a garden where the lower part is surrounded by a large belt of conifer hedging or tall tress. My advice here would be to work on the good lawn area and create another feature where the failing lawn is, for example an additional seating area.

If you're planning to sow a new lawn, make sure you purchase the correct seed mixture for your growing conditions. There are lots of lawn seed mixtures to choose from, including ones specially mixed for shady areas and areas that are prone to excessive moisture or drought.

Similarly, turfs are now available in drought-tolerant, shade-resistant varieties. When ordering new turfs you should discuss your growing conditions with the nursery staff and ensure that the turf they stock is suitable. Many garden centres simply order a standard one-type-fits-all turf that may not be appropriate for your garden. If this is the case, seek out a specialist turf supplier on the internet or via the *Yellow Pages* or similar, and ask them for details of local stockists.

BARBECUE AREA

When considering whether or not to include a barbecue area in your new garden there are a number of options available, from building a purpose-built traditional barbecue structure to simply deciding on where to store a portable barbecue.

One of the main advantages of opting for a portable barbecue is that there is now an enormous range to choose from. Where previously there were only solid-fuel barbecues available, you can now choose from electric, gas, solid fuel and traditional pre-built brick structures that you simply erect in your garden. In my experience, opinions among my customers and workshop participants have been as varied as the options available. Some people are adamant that the only way to get the real barbecued food taste is to opt for a brick-built barbecue complete with chimney. Others disagree, citing convenience, easy maintenance and portability as being the overriding factors in them choosing a gas barbecue, which when not in use is stored in either the garage or garden shed.

Certainly my own working experiences seem to support the latter view that portable is better, as I'm asked to demolish and remove more solid barbecue structures than construct them. I think the main advantage of the portable option is that you can tuck it away out of sight when it's not in use, which leaves you with a relatively larger seating or patio area – particularly important if your garden is small and space at a premium.

If space isn't an issue and you're still undecided as to whether or not to opt for a brick-built structure, then my advice would be to include a barbecue area in your garden plan. The advantage of this is that you can use this area initially for a portable barbecue and if you later decide brick is the way to go then you've already the space ready to take it.

When deciding on where to position your barbecue or barbecue area, consider carefully all the factors that could impact on its success. My own view is that barbecues are better situated somewhat off the main seating area and as close to the outside tap and kitchen window as possible. You should also consider which way the prevailing wind blows, as the last thing you want is to have to sit and suffer a constant stream of smoke blowing in you and your fellow diners' faces.

When I've built barbecue areas I've tended to position them in areas of the garden that are difficult to know what to do with. For example, one of my clients had a sloped area directly outside his utility room. The sheer drop in levels from the main footway to the base of the slope made it impossible to lay lawn or do much with it. In the end I came up with an innovative solution where I created a platform constructed using railway sleepers where my client could situate his barbecue. Its low-lying position meant there was no risk of smoke or fumes blowing up to the patio area above, while the whole arrangement allowed for the barbecue chef still to be able to converse with his guests while cooking.

PATHWAYS

Not only are pathways essential for easy navigation round your new garden, but they are also, depending on where you position them, a great way of creating interest and surprise.

While every garden will be different in terms of layout and size, most gardens tend to have their pathways laid out in largely unimaginative ways. The reason for this is that house builders want to make things as simple for themselves as possible. Seldom is any thought given to the layout of the garden, and the most common arrangement is simply to run the path round the perimeter of the house and then down one side closest to the boundary fence to end when it reaches the back fence or wall. Depending on the size of the garden, the pathway may then continue along the rear boundary and up the other side of the garden, effectively framing it, with the result that regardless of how much you fiddle and move other features, your proposed new garden will always look somewhat square and unimaginative.

When it comes to making dramatic changes to the layout of your garden, working on a new route for your pathways is a great way to break free of the mundane.

Obviously not everyone will be in a position, financial or otherwise, to dig up existing footpaths and reroute them through different parts of the garden. But for those wanting a complete new look for their garden, pathway repositioning should be considered.

Often it's not necessary to dig up existing structures. You could simply add an additional pathway that winds its way though your main lawn area – particularly appropriate for the long, narrow garden plot. Rather than dig up the existing boundary pathways you could disguise them with containers planted with tall shrubs interspersed with vibrant flowers. Another relatively inexpensive way of disguising existing straight pathways is to extend and curve the boundary borders out from the long pathway. The border is then planted in front of the pathway while the existing pathway is covered over with containers between which you can add soil, thus disguising the path. As soon as the border matures you won't be able to see the pathway anymore.

GAZEBOS AND ARCHWAYS

Gazebos and archways aren't just for breaking up a long, boring garden. They can also be used to create entrances for other areas, for example leading into a vegetable or herb garden that is out of sight of the main garden. Another advantage of adding a gazebo or archway into your garden is that you can use the frame as an additional area for growing climbers, roses and all those shrubs that prefer to grow upright.

When considering where to position your feature, make sure you leave enough room between the archway and what's behind to allow for whatever it is you're growing up it to spread without being blocked by other shrubbery. For example, climbers such as clematis will grow out considerably as well as climbing upwards along the trellising. It's important therefore to allow them room to breathe and you'll also be rewarded with a denser coat of flowers when in season. Lots of room also makes for easier pruning and cutting back.

As well as positioning the feature in the centre of the garden to break up certain areas, you can also successfully incorporate gazebos and archways to add colourful interest and soften an otherwise angular corner.

Whether you're planning to buy a ready-made structure or build your own, you should ensure that your entrance area is as tall and wide as possible. A common mistake is to create an entrance with similar dimensions to an average doorway. The problem here is that as your climbers or foliage grow, the entrance gap narrows considerably, and if you're growing something thorny like climbing roses, you run the risk of injury every time someone walks through. So make sure you allow as wide and as high a gap as possible – certainly no less than 7ft in height with the gap wide enough to accommodate people, encroaching foliage, wheelbarrows and all those things you're going to push through it.

WATER BUTTS AND GREY WATER SYSTEMS

With the seemingly perpetual hose-pipe bans in parts of the UK, it makes sense to include somewhere in your new garden provision for at least one water butt. Obviously the position of your water butt will very much depend on where your existing downpipes are and how visible you want your water butt to be. Personally I like to include more than one water butt in my garden plan and to situate one on the patio area, which can be used for watering container pots and hanging baskets, another two on either side of the property, both of which can be used to water the main rear gardens, and if possible another to the front of the property for watering the front garden.

If the idea of having something that resembles a plastic bin somewhere in or around your property doesn't appeal very much, there are lots of ways of disguising them. For example, you could box them in using either brick or wood, use trellising on which you can grow flowering creepers, or simply paint them the colour of your property so that they blend in with the over-all building line.

A number of companies are now offering irrigation systems that reuse your 'grey water'. Grey water is the water that comes from your bath and sinks. The system works in that it filtrates the water removing any soap or bleach elements, thus making it suitable for watering everything in your garden.

You don't have to go to the relatively large expense of having a specialist system installed. You could simply opt for the relatively cheap and easier to self-install system whereby you connect a flow valve to your waste water downpipe (not toilet water) and add some additional piping, which then allows the flow of waste water to fill your water butt. The advantage is that your water butt will remain full and useful in times when there is little or no rainfall. Some gardeners argue that the water taken from the bath, shower and upstairs wash basins is unsuitable to use unless filtrated. My own view based on my own experiences of using grey water is that this isn't the case. And far from the water causing any noticeable damage to our shrubs and plants, they seemed to perform all the better for the experience of reusable water.

Whatever you decide, give some thought to including either a natural (water butt) irrigation system or one where you recycle your grey water. It's one positive way of avoiding the unsustainable reliance on water companies to provide water for your garden, and if you have a water meter fitted to your property you could well benefit from savings on your water bills.

BIRD BOXES

Sadly, natural bird-nesting areas are in decline. Modern living destroys natural hedgerows in favour of fencing or brick structures, builds houses in areas that were once home to birds and wildlife, and promotes garden designs that don't include any trees or even large bushes where birds can nest. Therefore it's great if you can include in your new garden design some provision for our feathered friends.

When it comes to deciding on a suitable place to position your bird box, you don't have to worry too much about height. Neither is it necessary for you to have a tree in your garden. You can attach your bird box to the walls of your home, garden shed or garage. Obviously the best position will be one where the birds can come and go free from fear of attack from any ground animals, including domestic cats. If there is an area that affords natural protection from the wind, rain and direct sunlight then great. If not, try to position the box somewhere that's not going to be in full sunshine and where it will be as sheltered as possible. When affixing your bird box, position it tilting slightly forwards so that it deflects the heaviest of the rain from entering. Make sure also that the position allows for the most direct flight path.

How many boxes you erect will depend mostly on the size of your garden and your personal preferences. Many species of bird are territorial and will not nest alongside other neighbours. Those that will include the tree sparrow. So if space and preference allow, you could erect a number of bird boxes in and around your garden and property. If you do this, you'll be rewarded with a most amazing and interesting natural addition to your garden, where you will be able to watch the comings and goings often very close up.

Even in our tiny courtyard garden we've erected a bird box on our rear garden wall nestled in among the foliage of a large laurel and the feature is the focus of much welcome activity.

BIRD FEEDERS

As well as bird boxes, bird feeders make interesting features to hang from trees, shrubs and walls. You can also buy purpose-built feeder stations where you simply leave food out for the birds. Similar to bird boxes, make sure you situate your feeder as far away as possible from the threats of cats.

The period for feeding birds is generally from November to April, as it is during the winter when the ground is most likely to be frozen and wet that birds find looking for their own food most difficult. It is said that if you feed the birds during this period they'll reward you in spring with their singing. Certainly this has been our experience.

COMPOST AREAS

Just as introducing water butts into your garden and recycling your grey waste water can reduce your water bills and improve the health and quality of your garden, making your own compost can save you money and reduce your reliance on landfill for your waste.

If you're planning to make your own compost then you'll need to give some thought as to where you position the composter. While most people tend to position their compost bin as far away from their home as possible – usually down the end of the garden somewhere – this means you possibly have a very long trek to get to feed it. The advantage of situating it away from the main home and outside living area is that you avoid the potential for bad smells and the general unpleasantness that goes with having something that is perpetually decaying. You could then leave a container outside your kitchen door to fill up with the composting ingredients as listed below, and then at convenient intervals empty it at the main compost heap.

Contrary to popular belief, grass cuttings aren't the only thing you can put on your compost heap. You can include all sorts of general household waste that you would normally throw out, including cardboard, egg boxes, paper towels, tea bags, coffee grounds, dead flowers, etc. You can also include fruit and vegetable peelings, spent bedding plants, leaves, soft pruning cuts and sawdust. However, newspapers and glossy magazines are best avoided, as are meat and fish.

Making compost is relatively straightforward and involves you simply heaping all the above into one large lidded container where the mixture eventually rots. You can also help it on its way by occasionally turning the heap with a fork so that the materials already rotting get mixed in with the rest of the green waste. If the mixture is dry, add some water.

Generally the process can take anywhere from a couple of months to a year before it's ready to be used in your garden. But don't let this put you off. Making your own compost is an excellent way of reducing the amount of waste materials you would ordinarily have to dispose of and once your compost is ready you don't have to buy in other composts.

WOODPILES

Include a woodpile somewhere in your garden if you want to attract wildlife. Hedgehogs and field mice are just two of the animals that love to nest and overwinter in a nice, snug woodpile. The best place to situate your woodpile is away from your property and if possible in an area that's not generally used by the pedestrian traffic. Thus the area is not threatening and allows for wildlife to come and go without fear of human interference. Sides of garden sheds, tucked away behind outhouse buildings or out of sight near the compost heap are just some suitable locations. Obviously you should avoid disturbing the pile during the autumn and winter periods.

OUTDOOR LIGHTING

By installing outdoor lighting you can create magnificent nocturnal garden scenes throughout the year. Kaleidoscopes of colour can be created relatively simply using modern, easy-to-install, off-the-shelf garden lighting systems.

You can also opt for my favourite – solar-powered lighting. The advantage of solar-powered lighting is that you get to enjoy nightime lighting by harnessing daytime natural light. The other and often overlooked benefit of solar-powered lighting is that you don't have to worry about running cabling and wires to your lights. Most lights come on a spike, which you simply push into the ground wherever you want them.

Depending on your requirements and personal preferences, a possible disadvantage is that the lighting tends not to be as bright as electric lights, but you could use both systems side by side and thus reduce your dependence on electricity while enjoying the benefits of solar-powered lighting.

Where you decide to position your lights will be a matter of personal preference. For example, some of my clients have included discreet lighting along their pathways, which gives a really magical feeling at night as well as allowing for romantic, nocturnal strolls down to the secluded summerhouse at the rear of the garden. Lighting in or around a water feature can create spectacular effects, particularly if a variety of colours are used.

The trick to creating great outdoor lighting is to enjoy the effect of light without seeing the lights themselves. By hiding your lights among foliage, water or features, you avoid the possibility of replicating something like you would see in a public car park.

When it comes to installing your lights you should follow the instructions that come with the set. Most electrical lighting systems will involve laying lengths of cabling through your garden, so you'll need to be careful where you position them. It's not uncommon for gardeners to slice through cable while digging over borders or forking the lawn. There are all sorts of things you can do to help avoid this kind of accident, including laying the cable in a protective piping, which is then buried.

Depending on the system you choose and how elaborate you want your lighting to be, you may need to employ an electrician to install it for you or at the very least inspect your work and ensure that it not only conforms to building regulations but, more importantly, is safe.

◆ CHECKLIST ◆

- ◆ Once you've decided what you want to include in your new garden, you need to decide where it's all going to go.

- ◆ Choose your locations carefully. For example, an incorrectly positioned pond will cause you problems in the future.

- ◆ When deciding on a position for something, don't forget to consider how this position will impact on everything else in your garden.

- ◆ Consider the environmental benefits of making your garden wildlife-friendly.

- ◆ Be especially careful when positioning bird boxes and feeders to make sure the birds are safe from other animals such as cats.

- ◆ Don't forget to consult your Local Authority and ask whether or not you need planning permission for any proposed new structures.

- ◆ Ensure when planning outdoor lighting that you protect the cabling from being accidentally sliced through.

8

GETTING READY TO START ON YOUR PROJECT

SETTING A BUDGET

Before you even lift a shovel or pull on your Wellingtons, you should set a provisional budget for your project. This country is littered with half-finished gardening projects, which have come to an abrupt end through a lack of money or time, or a combination of both.

The benefit of setting a provisional budget before you begin any work is that you can at least have some degree of confidence that the project you're about to embark on is achievable. One of the biggest drawbacks of television and magazine garden makeovers is that they rarely give any indication of what sorts of costs are involved. Unfortunately this results in many novice gardeners rushing into a project without giving costs enough consideration. Problems arise when you come to order your new patio and discover that the costs are completely out of your budget, even if you do the job yourself.

Within the scope of this book it would be impossible for me to cost every item that you might need for your new garden. Instead, what follows is a guide to making you more aware of the additional costs that might not be readily apparent.

COSTING HARD FEATURES

Patio areas and pathways/driveways

Costs associated with patio areas might include:

- Cost of new paving slabs.
- Cost of excavating the site where the new patio will go and if necessary disposing of any spoil.
- Cost of materials you will need in addition to the paving slabs, which will include cement, sand and possibly lengths of wood to create a construction frame. If you're constructing a concrete pathway, you'll need to construct a wooden retaining frame, and the costs of the wood will depend on the length and width of your pathway.
- Shovels, trowels, gloves and eye-protection wear.
- Hire of any equipment. Mixing cement by hand can be extremely hard work and generally speaking you'd do well to hire a cement mixer.
- Tarpaulin covers to lay over your new or part-laid patio to protect the area while you're working or overnight from inclement weather, including rain and frost.

Boundary fencing

Costs associated with erecting boundary fencing might include:

- The fencing panels.
- Sand and cement or a ready-made 'postcrete' to fill in around the fencing posts.
- Colour or stain if you're going to paint the fence a different colour from the standard manufacturer's weatherproof staining.
- Disposal costs of any old fencing. Note that owing to the weatherproofing stain, fencing is not a product that can be easily recycled.
- If you are erecting one where one has not previously existed, you should consider hiring a specialist hole-borer. The machine will bore a suitable hole in which you can place your fence post. All you then have to do is concrete around the base for stability.
- If you are repairing or altering an existing fence, you may be unable to dig up the existing concrete base. A popular alternative is to purchase a repair spike, which is basically a cup for holding the new fence post with a 'spike' for slipping down onto the existing remains of the rotting post.

As you can see, replacing or repairing an existing fence isn't just about how much the fence panels are going to cost you. Similarly, when it comes to patios and pavements you need to be aware of all the potential costs you face in addition to purchasing your paving slabs.

What's the best way of working out provisional costings?

When it comes to working out the potential costs of hard features, the best place to go is one of the recognised builder's merchants yards. Most of these businesses are open to members of the public and not just builders or landscapers. The advantage of buying your goods from these centres is that the staff are generally trained to sell building products. They're not just shelf-stackers or retail assistants, and because they spend their working lives dealing with the building trade, their knowledge and expertise is vast, especially when it comes to what type of materials you should use.

I often get approached by DIY garden landscapers who on completing a project find that they've overestimated the quantities of materials purchased. Usually it's sand they're trying to offload. When I ask them what type of sand they have, they look at me amazed and some even get quite angry about it: 'It's SAND!', they say. But there are a number of different sands available for example sharp sand, building sand and play sand. Each sand is suitable for a different application. I dread to think how many patios and pathways have been laid using the wrong type of sand.

So when choosing and working out quantities of hard materials, it pays to take professional advice and visit building centres, as opposed to relying on multi-retailers who sell everything from lawn seed to paving slabs.

The information that a building centre assistant will require from you in order to give an accurate quotation will include:

◆ The size of the patio/seating area/path that you are planning to construct.
◆ The type of paving stones. If you cannot work out the quantity of slabs you need, ask the sales staff. Even if you have worked out your quantities, it's always a good idea to ask the staff to double-check them. Don't feel too proud to do this. Overorder your materials and you waste money; underorder and you won't be able to finish the job.

◆ Describe your site conditions and ask for their advice on what sand/cement ratio you should use. If the area is particularly prone to waterlogging or damp, take along a photo and ask them what they think you should do to help alleviate the problem.

The other advantage of using specialist building centres is that they will usually deliver your materials either free of charge if you spend over a certain limit, or for a small additional fee. Many also have a returns policy, so if you do overorder materials they will accept them back and issue either a credit or a refund for your purchase. Make sure when placing your order that you ask about free delivery and returns policy.

Here is an example of a provisional working budget that one of my workshop attendees recently completed.

Description of proposed garden makeover: Lay a new patio seating area outside French doors, create a small new lawn and choose a new garden furniture suite.

New patio	£800
New lawn	£650
Additional garden furniture	£350
Planting budget	£300
Hiring in specialist help	£500
Contingency	£250
Total budget	£2850

As you can see, the anticipated costs are just shy of £3,000. For that money all you're getting is a new lawn and patio together with some garden furniture, and already the costs are relatively high. These figures do not include any labour as the person was planning to undertake all the work themselves.

So before committing yourself to any final plans, make sure you have a fairly accurate idea of how much it's all going to cost. The advantage of working out and setting budgets is that you can then alter them as necessary. For example, if the overall budget available in the above illustration was £2,000, you could decide whether on not you really needed the new furniture and lawn. The reason I suggest going with the patio is that this is the largest piece of the proposed project in terms of time and money,  and it would make sense to get this done and out of the way first. When time and money allow, you could then lay a new lawn. Or instead of investing in a new lawn, you could simply reseed or improve on the existing lawn.

COSTING SOFT FEATURES

You are also going to have to budget for soft features. In my experience it's here particularly that the best-laid plans go to pot. For example, well-meaning but inexperienced gardeners visit the garden centre on a Saturday morning and get swept away by all that's on offer.

The only successful way to shop for soft features is to go armed with a shopping list and stick to it rigidly. If something takes your eye and you're tempted to buy it, don't. Simply make a note of it. When you return home, check how and where it would go and grow in your new garden scheme. If there's an obvious and immediate place it could go and you've got the budget available, then plan a return trip to the garden centre. It's important to get out of the habit of wandering around garden centres buying whatever it is that takes your fancy. Far better for you to preplan your purchases and buy only those plants and shrubs that you have previously researched and are sure will survive and thrive in your new garden.

When working out provisional costings for your project you should first work out how much money you've got available to spend. Be honest with yourself here. There's little point in working out some great new garden plans if all they will ever be is exactly that. By working out how much money you have available to spend before finalising what you're going to spend it on, you can avoid lots of unnecessary stress and frustration.

CREATING A SCHEDULE OF WORKS

Once you've set your budget and worked out what you're going to do in your new garden, you're ready to create a Schedule of Works.

Regardless of the size of your proposed garden makeover or creation, you should always sit down and draw up a Schedule of Works. Basically what you're doing is creating a timetable, a workable 'to-do' list, with the added benefit that it gets you thinking about areas that perhaps up until now you have overlooked. For example, what will you do if as part of your work you have to remove a section of your boundary fence, which will leave your garden open. How are you going to keep your children or pets in and outsiders out?

Although not a definitive list, your Schedule of Works should include:

1. A start date for your project and, just as importantly, a finish date.
2. Those works you will need to undertake first.
3. The materials you will have to order and where you're going to store them until needed. Bear in mind that the only available areas for storing materials may well be in the garden you're planning to make over.
4. The impact of any ongoing works on your home life.
5. An actual timetable from which to work.

THE IMPORTANCE OF START AND FINISH DATES

The first and I believe the most important thing to get right in your Schedule of Works is to set start and end dates for the project. The advantage of this is that it gets you thinking about how long the project will actually take, as opposed to starting off with no idea. One of the greatest dangers I believe you face is running out of energy and motivation. What starts off as an exciting project can soon, if you're not careful, become a dreaded chore that you find reasons to avoid. By setting your start and finish dates before you begin, you can at least plan your life in advance, warning friends and relatives that for the next so many days, weeks or months you're going to be busy working on your new garden.

Another not immediately obvious advantage of setting start and finish dates is that you have to work out how long you think each job will take. When attendees at my workshop have done this they've often decided that the length of time needed to complete the project is greater than they can allow, so instead they have revised their projects to become more achievable. Obviously it's far better to make these decisions prior to starting than to alter plans half way through your project.

IDENTIFYING WHAT NEEDS TO BE DONE FIRST

It might seem obvious, but a surprisingly large number of people get this part very wrong. For example, I've had clients who have asked me to lay a new lawn and then once I've finished they've had builders in to put up a new conservatory. The result has been that all my hard work and my client's money has been wasted as the builders have used the new lawn as a place to lay out their materials and tools. So it's important that when deciding what to do first, you work out what the implications for the rest of the project are likely to be.

Although every project will be different and each new garden will have its own exacting requirements, I find the following system works best:

1. Start off by working on what you want to get rid of, and get all your clearance, cutting down, demolishing, etc. completely out of the way before you do anything else.
2. Build any hard features. Draw up a list of all the things you have to build, including fencing, pathways, patios, ponds, etc. Within this list prioritise what to do first. I always start from the outside and work my way in. So if fencing is required, I begin with that and then move on to paths and then finally lay the patios.
3. Only when you have completed all your hard feature building should you start on the soft features. Don't be tempted to rush in and start planting borders before you have your new fence up. Or laying a new lawn before the pathways and patios are in. You need to be patient and wait until all the solid frameworks are in and completed, including any painting or staining that might be needed.

4. Now draw up a soft feature schedule with its own priorities list. Again I always start from the outside and work in. Therefore begin by planting borders and trees and work in towards the building lines. The final soft planting that should be done is, if required, to lay the new lawn. Once the lawn is laid you can sit back and enjoy the new garden without having to trample over all your hard work.

THE MATERIALS YOU WILL NEED AND WHEN

It's unlikely that you will be able to walk into your local builder's merchants or garden centre and simply fill your trolley with everything you need. So you're going to have to work out which materials to order and when you'll need them in your garden. A distinct disadvantage of having everything arrive all at once is that you cannot immediately check each slab or other materials for damage. You're also faced with the problem of how to store everything while you get on with the work.

So it's a good idea to plan phased deliveries of your materials. If you plan to order all your materials from one source, make sure you order and pay for them straight away so you can get bulk purchase discounts. Then negotiate for the materials to be delivered in accordance with your Schedule of Works. Most builder's merchants are happy to do this and indeed are used to working this way. However, garden centres who primarily cater for the public may not be too pleased when you ask them.

IMPACT OF THE PROJECT ON YOUR LIFESTYLE

This is when pre-planning and contingency come into their own. For example, if you're garden is an important play area for your children or pets, you're going to have to plan safe alternatives for them while you undertake the work. In my experience nothing is more attractive to children than the sight of dad's 'toys' in the form of cement mixers, mini-diggers, stone-cutters, etc. So you really do need to give safe alternatives some serious thought before you start your project.

With a well-thought-out Schedule of Works you can cover all these issues before you start. For example, if you're going to lay a new patio then obviously the last thing you're going to want is your pets and children trampling over the freshly laid mortar base or slabs. With forward planning you could arrange for the children and pets to take a short break with a relative or friend, even if it's just for the day, to let you get on with your work uninterrupted.

Whenever I undertake any garden construction I always serve notice on the homeowner that pets and children are not allowed into the garden while I'm working. Occasionally I've had clients complain about this. Under such circumstances, I cannot operate safely and if I cannot be assured of a clear working space I won't undertake the work. *Children, pets and machinery don't go together, so make sure you deal with this in your Schedule of Works.*

BAD WEATHER – AND HOW TO CONTINUE WORKING WHEN IT'S RAINING

It's quite common to plan to lay your new patio on a certain day, only to wake to find that heavy rain has made the job impossible. Although unwanted, such situations aren't altogether unexpected, and therefore a contingency should be built into your plans.

The way I get round the threat of rain is to erect a cheap plastic gazebo available in most garden centres over the patio area where I will be working. It's a great way of ensuring a dry environment for your work without it costing you a fortune. You can also use the gazebo for any other work you need to do.

Contingency planning is everything. Don't be surprised or annoyed when bad weather interferes with your project. Provided you pre-plan for the eventuality, you should be able to continue with your work. If you cannot tackle one particular job, then find another one to work on. Personally I don't mind working in the rain. I quite enjoy the feeling of being outdoors in all weathers. Obviously it won't appeal to everyone.

SETTING A TIMETABLE

If you've followed every step so far, you should now have a timetable for your works. Providing you approach your project mindful of the logistical implications of what you're doing, then the chances are that everything will go according to plan. The only reason that the common, and I believe altogether unnecessary, 'Sods law' comes into play is as a direct result of a lack of project management.

While initially you may be tempted to rush into your project and adopt a 'we'll cross that bridge when we come to it' approach, you will soon find that you are wasting time and money. If you run your project as a professional would, you'll not only enjoy the process far more but you will also save time and money.

◆ CHECKLIST ◆

- ◆ Before lifting a spade, make sure you set a budget for your project.

- ◆ Once you've worked out some provisional costings for your project, you'll need to create a Schedule of Works.

- ◆ A Schedule of Works is necessary so you can plan a timetable for your project and if necessary arrange phased deliveries of your materials.

- ◆ Generally speaking, hard features are created first, and soft features last.

- ◆ Consider the impact on your lifestyle of the project. Make practical plans for such things as making sure your garden is safe for children while the works are underway.

- ◆ Bad weather is nothing new. Plan for it and consider ways that you can continue working in the rain, for example by erecting temporary gazebos over patio areas.

9

PROBLEMS, PRACTICALITIES AND POSITIONS

IDENTIFYING PROBLEMS – PERCEIVED OR OTHERWISE

I'm putting this section here as it's important that from now on you start planning your garden as a professional would. The benefit of doing this now is that you can work out a list of potential problems and then start on how you are going to tackle them. What follows is by no means a definitive list, but more of a thought-provoking list that will hopefully get you thinking like a pro.

THE AREAS WHERE PROBLEMS MOST OFTEN OCCUR

The four main problem areas you need to be aware of are:

1. Neighbours.
2. Suppliers.
3. Seasonal problems.
4. Personal problems.

Neighbours

In my experience most neighbours pose no problem and most will be more than supportive. However, there are those who won't. I've turned up at jobs to find neighbours deliberately blocking the areas where we need to park our trucks and then demand to see a copy of the planning permission for the garden shed we've arrived to erect or the patio we're about to construct. I've even had one couple demand to know exactly what their neighbours were having done as they were concerned it might be 'too vulgar and not in keeping with our own beautiful garden'.

Another source of potential neighbour dispute is when you're planning to remove some long-standing feature such as a tree, hedge, wall, etc. There is now legislation in place regarding boundary hedges and how high they should be. At the time of the writing, this legislation is still in its infancy with few case law examples that I can share with you. So my advice is this: if you are planning to plant a boundary hedge, first get a copy of the guidelines of what you can and cannot do from your local council offices. Regardless of what you're planning, hedge or otherwise, it's always a good idea to let your immediate neighbours know. Prior to undertaking any landscaping work, I always recommend our clients go and tell their neighbours that we're about to descend. The benefit of this is that the majority of people will be flattered you've bothered to tell them at all.

Suppliers

One of my major headaches is suppliers. While some are very good and keen on customer service, many are not. Estimated delivery dates are usually just that, and far too often the dates get put back to such an extent that either the client cancels the order or we have to change suppliers and start again. The main problem is that so much material is now imported from abroad. Stone and wood, for example, often come from Eastern European countries, so your delivery is dependent on lots of factors outside your control.

The other problem you face once you get over the delivery stage is the variable quality of the goods. For example, when we've ordered decking boards from certain suppliers in the past we've found as many as one in three unusable because they have been kinked, split or otherwise damaged. You can imagine what this problem can do to your works schedule.

The ways to minimise these sorts of frustrations are first of all to choose reputable suppliers, and second, to try where possible to choose materials that are readily available and in stock. Don't simply ask them if they always have a material in stock, because they'll most likely say yes. Instead give them an idea of the quantities you're looking for and then ask them how much of a lead time they would need if and when you came to order. If they glibly say they always have the material in stock, then ask for it right there and then and put them to the test.

A final word of caution when it comes to suppliers: beware of 'special offers' on certain materials. I recently visited our local DIY store to get some paint. While browsing through the stock a somewhat distraught man

came up to one of the staff and asked her where such-and-such a colour was. He waved an empty can in her face. She appeared to take some delight in telling him that they were out of that partic-  ular colour. 'But when will you be getting it in again?' he asked. 'We won't,' she said. 'It was on special offer because it was the end of the line. They're not making it anymore.' The customer became more agitated. 'But I'm half way through painting my lounge!'

There are two problems here. First, he'd underestimated his materials. A common but entirely avoidable mistake had he bothered to read the instructions on the back of the tin. However, his greatest mistake was that he didn't question why this paint was reduced to clear. A common tactic of DIY suppliers is that when something is discontinued they reduce the price to clear it. Conscious that earlier I advised you to start looking out for those bargains, you should do so with your eyes open and be ready to ask questions. For example, if you're planning to lay a new patio and you see a suitable stone at an irresistible price then you to need to make sure that it's available in sufficient quantities for you to complete your project. I'll show you later what's involved in doing this, but I think it's useful for you to be aware of the potential pitfalls as early as possible. Don't forget when ordering your slabs to include a few extra to allow for accidental breakage, etc.

Seasonal problems

I run my garden-planning workshops in autumn and over the winter. I do this because this is the best time for planning any garden makeover and also allows time to make necessary preparations and undertake any clearance work. Obviously, not everyone will be able to plan their new garden in the autumn, so don't worry too much about when you start. However, do be aware of the impact that the seasons can have on the work you're planning to undertake.

Autumn

Generally speaking, autumn is the time when gardeners tidy up, including seasonal pruning, cutting back encroaching foliages, removing spent summer bedding, applying compost to border areas and attending to lawn care, including scarification and aeration programmes.

If you're planning a new lawn then you can either prepare and lay it in autumn or preferably undertake preparations with a view to laying the new lawn early in the spring.

Autumn is also a useful time to sit back and have a good look at your garden in terms of colour and interest. For example, how much splendid autumnal colour can you see in your present garden? If your garden is overreliant on summer bedding and void of trees and mature shrubs, the chances are that by the time autumn comes around your garden is starting to look bland and uninspiring.

If you really want to see how impressive autumn can be in terms of colour and contrast, just spend a day walking, cycling or even driving through the countryside and find inspiration in the autumnal scenes. One of my favourite times of the year to go cycle touring is in the autumn. Often when I tell people this they're amazed as to why anyone would want to cycle when the weather is relatively poor compared to the summer or even spring months. But the fact is the countryside looks absolutely amazing at this time of the year, and nature is looking at its best and most interesting.

Some problems you might encounter in autumn are:

◆ Garden centres and nurseries turn themselves into Santa's grottos and stock their shelves with Christmas goods. Sourcing suitable materials at this time of the year can therefore be more difficult than in spring and summer.

◆ The weather can be inclement and at best unpredictable, making if difficult to get the right weather in which to build your hard features. For example, laying concrete bases for patios and the like can be troublesome. Strong winds can also play havoc when erecting fences and sheds.

◆ The end of October sees the clocks go back an hour and the usable daylight starts fading fast, something you need to take into account when planning. While in spring and summer you can work late into the evening, you don't get this luxury in autumn. If like many people you only have one day a week available for your project, then jobs will often get left unfinished waiting for the next weekend, providing the weather's suitable.

Some advantages to starting in autumn include:

◆ It is a great time to get to work on preparing the soil for future soft feature creation, for example, lawn and border preparations. Despite the weather it can also be a great time to get out in the garden and dig away the stresses of a week at work.

◆ Bulb planting. Autumn is the time to plant all those bulbs that will burst into colour and brilliance when spring comes. Even if you haven't got any border space planned or available for bulbs, stuff a few layers of them in your otherwise redundant pots and come spring you'll be amply rewarded.

◆ It can be a good time to get end-of-season bargains on garden furniture, sheds and the like.

◆ By spending time now getting the relatively heavy preparatory work out of the way, you're ready to start with the exciting task of building your new garden in spring.

Winter

Many gardeners write winter off as unsuitable for gardening, and even many of the gardening magazines portray winter gardening as being little more than browsing seed and plant catalogues and dreaming of spring. I don't agree with this. There are lots of things you can be getting on with in your garden over the winter, including:

◆ Repairing, replacing or renewing fences, walls, greenhouses, sheds, roofs, etc.
◆ Continuing or even starting preparatory works on future lawn areas, border areas, etc.
◆ If you've got your proposed garden plan completed, you can start on your project by undertaking any scheduled removal work, for example clearing out borders or removing dead, diseased or unwanted trees and other shrubbery.

One thing I wouldn't recommend you undertake in winter is to start working on your hard features. For example, anything involving concrete can be prone to frost damage. Under certain conditions frost can weaken cement and it's always best to leave this work until the frosts have cleared and the weather is kinder. Apart from this though, winter gardening can be great fun. If you've never spent a Saturday morning wrapped up working away in your garden under the winter sun, you don't know what you're missing! So don't let winter stop you from starting on your project. The secret is to choose those jobs that you can get on with readily and those that you don't really want to have to waste time on when the conditions are right for planting come the spring.

Spring

Spring is a magical time in the garden when everything starts to reawaken from winter slumbers. It's also a time of hope and inspiration for gardeners everywhere, when autumn preparations and winter work are finally rewarded.

Personally, I don't think there's a better time to create a new garden. You can do all sorts of things in spring, from laying new lawns to planting shrubs and trees and creating imaginative border planting schemes. With the prospect of better weather, longer daylight and an overall feeling of improved well-being, spring is the time to really get stuck into your project.

Potential seasonal problems are few but you should be aware of late frosts, which again can affect tender plants and damage concrete-based hard features. If you're laying new pathways or building concrete structures, you should always make sure you fully insulate them overnight to avoid the possibility of frost damage.

Summer

Ironically and somewhat contrary to what you might expect, summer is arguably the least favourable time to undertake a complete garden makeover project. If your project is already underway and you've prioritised your work schedule in the way I showed you in chapter eight, then you can easily take advantage of the summer months. However, the main drawbacks that you should be aware of if you're beginning your project in summer are:

◆ Unfavourable working conditions.
◆ Unfavourable planting conditions.
◆ Difficulty sourcing trades people and materials.
◆ Personal commitments.

Unfavourable working conditions

As I explained earlier, autumn and winter are best suited to undertaking preparatory work. For example, you can dig over areas of your garden in the autumn, which you can then leave unattended until spring. During this time your soil will benefit from any frosts which will break down compaction and any rain which will aid aeration, with the overall result of improving your growing conditions.

If you wait until summer to undertake preparatory works you may find that the soil is compacted to such an extent that you're unable to dig it over or carry out the necessary preparation because it now more resembles concrete than soil.

You may think that the hot dry weather would be great for laying that new patio, but don't forget that if it's too hot you're going to have to cope with your cement and mortar mixes curing and drying out too quickly.

If you are laying a new lawn you may find the weather is simply too hot to lay turfs. The problem with laying new lawn turfs is that you must keep them sufficiently moist. As soon as they dry out they shrink, causing problems when trying to lay them out as there will be gaps between each turf. Although you can remedy this to an extent by heavy watering, if the ground underneath the turfs is too dry the chances are that many turfs will not take root and simply dry up and die. Over the years I have experienced this on a number of occasions and now only ever agree to lay new lawns in spring or autumn.

Also don't underestimate that much of what you're trying to achieve may include some relatively heavy work. For example, lawn turfs by their very nature are heavy, as are paving slabs, and don't underestimate how potentially backbreaking shovelling and wheelbarrowing shingle and sand around your garden can be. When the weather is particularly hot these task are made all the more difficult. Indeed, there have been times when I've had to revise the work schedule as the conditions were too unfavourable to continue.

Unfavourable planting conditions

Although much will depend on what you're planning to plant or possibly transplant, generally speaking autumn and spring are the best months for planting. Again, conditions in summer can be unfavourable with an overall lack of moisture and the ground as solid as concrete. Increasingly throughout the country we're seeing blanket hose-pipe bans, thus making watering new border areas and lawns difficult. The advantage of planting outside summer is that although there still may be little rain, you will benefit from the natural overnight moisture caused by dew, etc.

Difficulty sourcing trades people and materials

It may be that your project will require you to employ specialist help. If this is the case then you need to be aware that August is a busy time for landscape contractors and builders. So if your project only involves them coming in to lay a relatively small patio or install a new water feature, the chances are they won't be available either through other work commitments or that they feel the job is too small and unprofitable for this time of year.

Similarly, when it comes to sourcing supplies you may find that at this busy time of the year many outlets have sold out of whatever it is you're looking for. This is especially true of materials such as decking, paving slabs, etc. As many of the companies that manufacture these products have high levels of staff absence owing to annual holidays, etc., this can have a considerable impact on availability. Many retailers also now source their decking timbers from Eastern European countries and supplies come by ship, making for long lead delivery times. While the helpful sales staff may optimistically say they'll 'have it in next week', this will depend on any number of factors outside their control.

Personal commitments

By its very nature we associate summer with relaxing, unwinding and making more out of our spare time. If you're working all week in a stressful environment it's nice to spend the long evenings and weekends on your favourite pastimes. If gardening isn't your favourite pastime, how will you feel when you're stuck labouring creating your new garden when you'd rather be out sailing, playing golf or walking?

Neither is working in the intense heat good for you or enjoyable. Personally I like to relax during my time off in the summer months and enjoy a wide range of activities as opposed to working on one thing. The advantage of spreading the work over the seasons is that you can plan your garden project around your lifestyle as opposed to making it the only thing in your life.

Obviously much will depend on your own lifestyle and how you would like to achieve your new garden. However, a common problem I've come across in my work is when couples or individuals have started a project at an unsuitable time of year and then abandoned it with a view to finishing at some undetermined time in the future. By planning to work at the relatively easiest times of the year you can minimise fatigue and the kind of 'wish I was doing something else' resentment that can so easily build up.

Again, summer is generally the time that friends and family visit, arrange functions, holidays away, etc., and trying to fit in a complete garden makeover during this time can be difficult to say the least. For example, you rise early on a Saturday morning intent on digging out the area where the new patio is going and then your friend rings inviting you to some irresistible event. If you decline, how happy will you be toiling away while you could be out there enjoying yourself? If you accept, what's this going to do for your relationship if your partner is out at work all day working under the impression that you're busy progressing the new garden? Then they arrive home to find you've gone fishing . . .

Whatever the season there's always something you can do. But wherever possible try to work with the seasons, taking advantage of natural assistance such as plenty of moisture in spring for plantings and sowing seeds and using the relatively dry summer for tackling those jobs that rely on good weather.

WHERE TO POSITION HARD FEATURES

When I run my workshops there are always a few students who feel that as soon as they arrive in the room they should start working on their design. Therefore it comes as a bit of a shock to discover that the first few hours are devoted to the subjects we've already covered in this book. One of the problems you potentially face if you simply grab the pad and starting working on a design is that what you come up with may not be suitable for your garden. That's why it's important to get the background information right first. By getting to know your garden as much as you can before attempting to redesign it, you substantially reduce the risk of coming up with a design that simply won't work given your garden's conditions.

Obviously you need to know what size your garden is and its aspect, but it is just as important for you to identify your own needs and also those who live in your household. Over the years I've seen too many gardeners turn a happy garden into something altogether too ornamental, where once-treasured pets find themselves no longer wanted and even children are banished to entirely unsuitable 'play areas'. If you haven't got pets or children at the moment then that's fine. However, if you create a new garden that's child unfriendly, for example with an enormous pond as its focal feature, you need to be sure that you intend to stay in your home in the long term as features like these can have an impact on resaleability. For example, I often get calls from new homeowners asking me to remove ponds, water features and rockeries, which they perceive to be a threat to their children.

Having now gone through in some detail your Lifestyle Questionnaire for you and your family and your survey for your garden, you're now ready to start thinking about what you want to put in your new garden and of course where these new features should go.

PROPORTION AND POSITION

As I've said previously, a good garden is one that flows effortlessly. There are no unsightly or impractical joints. For example, the lawn area is accessible for everyone, including whoever's job it will be to cut the grass; there are no flowerbeds that you have to abseil over to get to the seating area; and so on. This is not only good garden design, but common sense. Yet surprisingly I've worked in many gardens that have been supposedly professionally designed but lack any sense of natural flow.

Proportion

A common and easily made mistake is to choose a central feature for your garden, which could be a statue, building, water feature, lawn area, raised border or a soft feature such as trees, and then try to build your new garden around this feature. Occasionally this method might work out but generally it will be unsuccessful.

The feature you have chosen as your focal point will need to be of the right proportion to make the whole garden design work. For example, if your feature is too big for your garden, then it will have the effect of dwarfing everything around it. Too small and it will get lost in the wilderness.

By far the best way to approach choosing new features is to make sure when you visit garden centres you take with you the rough sketch of your garden, including all the crucial measurements. If you're planning to buy online or via armchair catalogue ordering, make sure you think measurements. Before you do anything, lay out your rough sketch so it's clear in your mind how much space you have available for what you're planning to buy.

Before finalising any intended purchase of features like rigid pond liners, benches, tables, chairs, summerhouses, birdbaths, sundials and so on, check their measurements. What looks big in a garden centre often looks miniscule in a large garden. Conversely what looks relatively unobtrusive in a garden centre or mail-order catalogue can appear completely out of place in a small garden. And when it comes to catalogue pictures or those on websites, it's difficult to judge the actual size without checking the measurements.

Remember that if you're looking for something large and you're planning to buy it by mail order, when it comes to delivery whatever it is you're intending to buy isn't going to fit through your letter box. Most mail-order companies charge additional carriage for oversized or especially heavy items, so if you don't see any additional carriage charges anywhere, recheck the item's description. A number of my clients have gone online and ordered features such as birdbaths and statues and subsequently been very disappointed when the item has arrived and turned out to be manu-factured from resin as opposed to the metal they thought it would be. When they've looked again at the catalogue or website they've noticed that this detail was included in the feature's description but they had failed to pick up on it.

◆ TIP ◆

Whatever you buy must fit your garden or it won't work in terms of your overall design.

I've always wanted to include some form of water feature in our courtyard garden. When I considered installing what appeared to be a relatively small raised pond I went home and with a ball of string laid out the diameter on the shingle. Then I erected a number of bamboo canes cut to the height the intended water feature would be so I could replicate its frame. As soon as it was in place I knew it was too big. And that was the smallest raised water feature available. So instead I went out and bought an aluminium water can, filled it with water and added some rushes plus some water-loving marginals hanging over the edge and it looked terrific until we got out new golden retriever pup who has his own ideas about how minimalist water features should look!

The important thing when it comes to proportion is to avoid rushing out and buying whatever it is you really like and then trying to fit it into your garden. Far better to look at your garden in terms of its size and aspect and find something that blends in with the overall site.

Position

It's crucial to the future success of your new garden that not just everything fits neatly into your design, but also that it is in the right position. Unless you've bought a house somewhere in rural France, it's unlikely that your garden will extend to anywhere near an acre. Certainly from my own experiences in running workshops and my gardening business, most gardens are now relatively small. If you've bought a new-build home, you'll probably find that your garden is on the small side. By their very nature the vast majority of town house and terrace house gardens will usually be no wider than the property itself.

While limited space isn't a problem in itself, it can mean that certain features will compete for garden space. For example, if when you've carried out your garden survey you've identified all the sunny areas in your garden, you may be disappointed that there are very few. Now let's imagine you love outside entertaining and want to create an area where you can dine outside in the sunshine. You also want to include a garden pond. Problems arise if in your garden there is only one area where the sun actually reaches. Not as uncommon as you might think. Obviously with only one such area available, you're going to want to position your entertaining area here. But what about your pond? Sunny areas are great for garden ponds, so clearly you have a conflict over which feature is going to benefit from the best position. If your garden is relatively large then this won't create a problem. However, if you have a small, narrow garden then you might have to rethink your whole pond idea in favour of a more suitable water feature.

The next chapter provides all manner of hints and tips on positioning hard and soft features.

◆ CHECKLIST ◆

- ◆ With careful planning, most problems can be avoided.

- ◆ Beware of the potential conflict that your project might bring with neighbours.

- ◆ You can reduce the likelihood of conflict by letting everyone know what you're planning.

- ◆ Whatever time of the year you start your project means that you'll have to work with the seasonal conditions at that time.

- ◆ Regardless of the season, there is always something you can be getting on with to keep moving your project forward.

- ◆ Proportion and position and are two very important concepts when it comes to designing your new garden.

10

STARTING WORK ON YOUR PROJECT

ADVICE ON EMPLOYING SPECIALIST HELP

Quite possibly there will be areas in your new garden where you will need to employ specialist help. Although this is more likely to involve erecting and building hard features such as walls, patios, pathways and fences, you might also have to bring in specialist companies to help with soft features. For example, if you're planning to cut back or fell any trees, I would recommend you employ the services of a tree surgeon. Nothing is more dangerous than an amateur on a ladder or even on the ground wielding a chain saw. Similarly, if you've already got a long boundary hedge containing a belt of conifers that you'd like reducing in height, then I'd recommend you bring in a specialist. *This sort of work is dangerous and should only be tackled with the right training and equipment.* In the past I've seen gardeners hacking away at conifers while perched precariously on a ladder with no safety harness or anything else to break their fall. If you work like this, one day your luck will run out.

CHECKS TO MAKE BEFORE EMPLOYING A CONTRACTOR

The easiest way to get a good contractor is to ask your neighbours. If you haven't got friendly neighbours you can ask, or if no one else you know can recommend anyone locally, here are some tips on how to source a quality landscaper or gardener.

Good gardeners are busy gardeners.

Were a prospective client to phone our landscape gardening business and ask for an estimate, I would usually arrange to meet them shortly after their call. However, when it comes to actually undertaking the work, there would generally be a three-month lead-in time before we could start on a major project.

So if you call a contractor, don't be put off if they tell you that while they can come round and give you an estimate in the next few days, it might be anywhere from six weeks to six months before they can start the work. It may be that you can work them into your project and if it's a relatively small job you're after they might be able to do it sooner. Whatever you do, you should be wary of the landscaper who not only can come round immediately and give you an estimate, but also, if you agree the price, can start work the next day.

Check advertisements carefully

When checking through advertisements in newspapers and magazines, don't be fooled into believing that the biggest advertisements are from the best and biggest contractors, because this is seldom the case. Very often it's the small box ad with the relatively modest presentation that can so often prove more promising. It's always a good sign when the landscaper includes their name in the advertisement and even better when their business name includes their full name. If a contractor is willing to pin their name to their work then that's a good indication that they will have some pride in what they do. Of course this may not always be the case, but generally speaking it's a good place to start. If when you phone you don't like the impression given, then politely finish the call and move on to the next one.

One thing you should always look out for before choosing a contractor is multi-ads from the same company. This is when you get one advertisement offering building service, another apparently unrelated ad offering rubbish clearance and another unrelated ad offering landscape gardening. The way to tie them all together is to look for the same phone number. It's good practice whenever you see an ad that attracts you to highlight the contact telephone number and check through other ads for the same number. You'd be surprised at how often you'll come across this. Don't be surprised if a company offering a complete bathroom installation then appears in the gardening section offering landscaping!

Get more than one estimate

Obviously it makes sense to get more than one estimate. But don't go overboard and don't try during your initial meeting with contractors to use the fact that you're intending to get other quotes as a bargaining tool. Personally, I value my business time. When I go to give an estimate, I'm giving a free service, which includes visiting a homeowner in their garden, discussing their requirements, offering advice and the benefit of my experience, and then working out how much it's going to cost them in terms of materials and labour. If during my meeting I get the impression that the homeowner is only interested in the lowest price, then I politely walk away. My advice is that during the first meeting you run through the checklist I've included below and leave price negotiations until you actually get a written estimate or quote.

Does the landscaper belong to a trade body?

Don't be put off if the landscape gardner isn't a member of a professional trade body.

For a variety of reasons, we decided not to renew our membership of the trade organisation that we belonged to. Whenever prospective clients contacted me, I always invited them not only to see examples of our finished work and speak with our clients, but also to come along and see us working.

So don't be afraid to ask to see examples of the contractor's work and also to speak to some of their customers. A professional company will have no problem with you doing this, and will probably invite you to do this without you asking.

Use your own judgement and wherever possible try to find someone who has been recommended. The following checklist is by no means definitive.

1. Don't be afraid to go with your 'gut' feelings. We all have them and in my experience nothing beats our inner intuition. If you suspect some-one isn't genuine then don't be tempted by lower prices or immediate availability.

2. Before you appoint a contractor be clear about what exactly is covered in the estimate. In my experience most problems arise not so much from contractors trying to have clients over, but more as misunder-standings on both sides from the word go. Prior to giving the go-ahead, invite your preferred contractor to return to your garden for a meeting to finalise exactly what you want and they can provide. Once you're happy, then give the go-ahead.

3. Telephone numbers say a lot about a business. My advice is if all they have is a mobile number then be wary. Likewise also be wary of those contractors who offer Freephone 0800 numbers. In my experience many of these divert to a mobile number and their owners don't actu-ally have a dedicated landline. Obviously this isn't always the case and there are many reputable businesses operating with Freephone num-bers, but do be sure to check them out.

4. Wherever possible, try to find someone you like. It's important to have a contractor who you get on with as opposed to someone who rubs you up the wrong way. Make sure you find someone who sees your project from your perspective.

5. When you're out and about, be on the lookout for a suitable contractor. The best way to see how they work is to watch them working.

WHAT TO DO IF IT ALL GOES WRONG

If despite your best efforts you choose a contractor and it's not working out, the most important thing is to bring whatever the problem is to their attention at the earliest convenience. Don't store up a list of problems and then hit them one day with them all. All this will do is inflame an already difficult situation. The secret to working successfully with a contractor on a project is to meet regularly to discuss progress and any difficulties. From a contractor's point of view, one of the most difficult things about working with homeowners is that they usually have no experience of managing a project and simply don't understand that what might seem a small alter-ation to them can actually have a major impact.

For example, I've worked on projects where at the last minute my clients have decided that they'd like a square patio as opposed to the previously quoted circular one. They have become irate when I've told them that it's too late as the paving slabs are already paid for, not to mention the fact that the rest of the garden is constructed around a circular patio. One lady called me 'inflexible' when I refused to instruct the delivery driver to take back the patio that she had already chosen, ordered and paid for.

CHOOSING THE RIGHT TOOLS

Before starting on your project you should have a look at what you have in the way of gardening tools. Nothing is worse than getting all fired up and ready to mix your cement for the new patio base only to find you don't have or can't find your spirit level. When I started my own gardening business I was forever misplacing tools, and it was only after my first year of trading that I realised the amount of time and money I was wasting both looking for and having to replace expensive tools.

What you need by way of tools will depend very much on what type of gardening project you're planning to undertake. For example, if you're planning a full-scale build including creating hard features, you're going to need more tools than if you're simply planning a soft-feature makeover. But before we get to what tools you will need, let's look first at you the gardener.

CLOTHING AND SAFETY WEAR

Gardening is a physically demanding job, which requires a certain degree of physical fitness and agility. Therefore, if you haven't recently undertaken any physical fitness and are in any way out of shape, I recommend you create a Schedule of Works that leads you gently into your new project.

A couple of years ago a prospective client asked me to provide him with an estimate to carry out some landscaping work. When I gave him my prices it was clear that my figures were somewhat out of his budget. However, he still wanted the work done, so he decided to undertake all the heavy clearance work himself and employ my business to build the hard features, which included a pathway and a pond. On the pre-agreed morning we arrived to find that most of the clearance work had not been undertaken and the client's tearful wife explained that he had had a stroke the previous week while working on the garden.

I tell you this story not to frighten you, but to prepare you. Gardening is often mistakenly viewed as some old guy in a flat cap pottering about with a barrow and a few leeks in his retirement. While this might be the case in some situations, building a new garden is anything but sedate. It requires a fairly high level of fitness, strength and stamina, so if you normally spend your working week behind a desk in an office, then start slowly. You will soon discover how tiring it can be filling a cement mixer with sand and cement, let alone barrowing it to wherever it needs to go.

Wearing the right clothes from the start won't necessarily make you fit, but it will make work easier. My preferred attire for undertaking landscaping work is as follows:

1. *Steel toecapped boots or Wellingtons.* Wellies with steel toecaps are now widely available. The traditional wellie offers no protection at all in the event that you drop something on your foot or stub your toe. The secret with toecapped boots is to wear them in gradually. Whatever you do, don't try to spend eight hours working in a new pair or you'll risk taking the skin off your feet.
2. *Heavy duty pair of loose-fitting combat-style trousers or similar.* The advantage with these is that they're robust enough not to let cement dust and the like through the fabric and risk contact with your skin. I also find the pockets useful and the loose-fitting material isn't restrictive for bending down.
3. *Polo-style T-shirt complete with collar.* If you're working in the sun make sure you turn up your collar to protect your neck. Unfortunately most crew-

necked T-shirts offer little or no protection for your neck area with the result that as you bend down to work you risk burning and sunstroke.

4. *Fleece top and jacket.* I love fleeces as they provide excellent warmth for working in the winter and are easy to take off and pull on as required. One of the things I always do whenever I take a break from working and am hot is to slip on a fleece over my T-shirt. You may think this is silly. However, one of the problems of working hard is that you tend to over-heat. Then when you take a break your body loses heat rapidly and you end up prone to a chill. By pulling on a fleece top or jacket you can minimise the risk of catching cold.

5. *Waterproof jacket and trousers.* I'm not too bothered about working in the rain, provided I have a decent set of waterproofs. The ones I use are those fluorescent council workman-style jackets you'll find in all good builder's merchants. Forget the DIY chains. Go to your local builder's merchants and buy a set of decent high-visibility waterproof clothing. You'll probably find that they're cheaper and better quality than any-thing being offered by the multi-retailers.

6. *Thermal underwear.* If you're starting your project in the depths of winter, thermal underwear is an excellent investment. Thermals are great not just for keeping you warm, but as they help retain body heat they also reduce the amount of energy your body has to use to keep warm. So you can work for longer, and be more comfortable. The trick when you start out in the cold is to be warm yourself. It's far easier to keep warm and stay warm than have to warm up and keep warm.

I cannot see any reason why the above list would be any different for ladies. I know a number of lady gardeners and landscapers who all swear by their combats, steel toecapped boots, fleeces and thermals.

ESSENTIAL TOOLS

Most gardening projects will need either some or all of the following items:

◆ *Quality Wheelbarrow.* Try to buy one of the deep barrows that are also narrow enough to fit through most garden gates. This is important as there are lots of heavy-duty barrows on the market that won't fit down the average side path or through a narrow side gate.

◆ *Spade and fork.* Buy a good-quality, heavy-duty spade and fork. Depending on how tall you are, try to buy a long-handled spade and fork to save breaking your back.

◆ *Shovel.* A shovel is distinct from a spade in that a spade is narrow, which makes it ideal for digging over borders, skimming off turfs, etc., while a shovel is wide and has a larger carrying capacity. Shovels are ideal for loading sand into cement mixers, shingle into barrows and so on. Generally speaking, they'll have a shorter handle than spades and are unsuitable for digging.

◆ *Builder's trowel.* If you're planning to do your own brickwork, lay a patio, or point or repoint paving, then a trowel is essential. It's also really useful as a general gardening tool for digging planting holes, filling compost into pots, transplanting small plants, etc. Obviously if you are using one for cement work, make sure it's clean enough to use as a gardening tool.

◆ *Spirit level.* Essential for any hard feature work and also for use when erecting sheds, fencing, etc.

◆ *Crowbar.* I find this tool invaluable. If you're planning to dig up any mature shrubs or small trees, you'll find a crowbar is excellent for levering things up. Don't use a spade or shovel to do this as they will either break or bend.

◆ *Rake.* A requirement for hard and soft feature creation. If you're laying a new lawn you'll need one to level out and till the soil. If you're laying a cement base, a rake held upside down is an excellent tool for levelling areas of cement. Plastic rakes are ideal for raking up leaves and clearing debris from a lawn without causing any damage.

◆ *Half-moon cutter.* Useful if you are redefining your lawn area from straight edges to curves, the half-moon edging tool is simple to use and gives brilliant, clear definition.

◆ *Clipping shears.* Quality is important here. There are lots of cheap clipping shears on the market that don't have very good blades, resulting in the leaves of whatever you're cutting being torn and shredded as opposed to being cut. This can make the foliage prone to die-back or pest infestation.

◆ *Secateurs.* Again buy the best you can afford. Invest in a good pair and they'll last you a lifetime provided you look after them. There's no fun to be had in using poor-quality cutting equipment.

SITE PREPARATIONS – MARKING OUT YOUR SITE

Once you have your thumbnail drawings, Schedule of Works and tools to hand, you're ready to begin your site preparations. Again, careful preparation will save you time and money, as well as giving you a final opportunity to make sure your overall design is going to work and fit neatly into your garden space.

Before you even cut back a shrub or scuff off some turf, you must first mark out the site with a non-toxic spray marking can, which are available from any builder's merchants. I use white lining for hard features and yellow lining for soft features. To mark out a site:

1. Work out the exact measurements of all hard features, including patio areas, footpaths, fencing lines, etc.
2. Draw each feature's outline on the ground using a white marker spray as a giant pencil. It's important when doing this that you draw the outlines of all features in one go so you can see exactly how the garden will look when completed.
3. Use the yellow marking spray to draw in the outlines of all the soft features, including lawn areas, planting areas, vegetable and herb areas, hedge outlines, and so on.

The time it takes to do all of this is considerable. However, I've yet to come across a client who when seeing the final outline in terms of size and proportion does not want to make at least one fairly significant alteration. It's amazing when you lay the proposed garden out on the soil how things will either look too big or too small.

A great advantage of spray outlining the new patio area is that you can actually place your table and chairs and anything else you're planning to house there to see if it all fits. Many pre-made patio areas are extremely small and will have difficulty accommodating four or five large chairs and a table on them. So the outline is really useful in determining what's right and what's not.

Always allow yourself a little time post-outlining to study the marking out in greater detail. Look at it from every room in your house, including upstairs. If possible I like to give clients at least a day and an overnight to study the whole thing before committing themselves to the final build design. The advantage with outlining is that there's no waste of money or time involved. And if you have got your measurements wrong, you still get an opportunity to put things right before it's too late.

Whenever I'm instructed to cut down trees or shrubs, I mark the ones that are to be cut down with either a ribbon or non-toxic spray. This way I can be assured that I'm felling the right trees. Obviously if you're undertaking the work yourself, you will know which shrubbery is going and what's staying. However, if you're employing a tree surgeon it's a good idea to mark those that you want felling. Mistakes that involve cutting down the wrong tree cannot be rectified, so it's worth being overcautious.

By working to a plan of what you're going to cut and what stays, you won't end up veering off it. In my experience it's easy to get carried away and before you know it everything, good and bad, wanted and unwanted, is gone.

A word on safety

When deciding to fell anything larger than a mature shrub you should really employ specialist help, preferably in the form of a qualified tree surgeon. Thankfully you cannot easily hire chain saws these days. Unqualified people should not use chain saws under any circumstances, whether they be of the petrol or electric variety. The speed at which a petrol chain saw operates is such that you could remove your leg before you knew about it. If you really want to fell your own trees, then go on an approved chain saw course. There are courses for ground work and height work. It's also illegal to use certain chainsaws for ground use and visa versa. While this might seem unnecessarily complicated, there are good reasons for this. So don't be misled by anyone into thinking that it's a doddle to fell your own trees. It's not. It requires specialist training and it's beyond the scope of normal everyday gardening. Please don't put yourself at risk for the sake of saving money. I've worked with chain saws and they really are frightening. In untrained, incapable hands, they're lethal.

UNDERTAKING CLEARANCE WORK

The secret here is to put the emphasis on recycling rather than disposing!

In my experience, clearance work is one of those areas that quickly spirals out of control if left unchecked. For example, if you're cutting back lots of shrubs, brambles, foliage, etc., you'll quickly find that the space the branches take up is enormous. Even if you try to pack them into large rubble sacks, the boot of your car or a small trailer, the chances are you won't get more than a few branches in at any given time. The trick here is to shred your clippings using a machine. Before rushing off to a DIY store to buy one, you should instead visit your local tool and machinery hire shop as what you're looking for is something far heavier duty and capable of gobbling up larger branches. Professional hire centres will show you exactly how to work the machinery, deliver it to your garden and provide you with all the safety clothing and accessories needed to do the job.

Rather than having sacks and trailer-loads of unruly branches and cuttings, you'll be left with quantities of excellent woodchip mulch mixture, which you can then spread over your new planting areas to encourage growth and retain moisture.

When getting rid of unwanted hard features, for example old paving slabs, you should consider recycling them even if you're not immediately able to use them. For example, if you have an allotment holding near where you live the chances are you'll find lots of gardeners keen to take the off your hands as they can use them for creating hard-standing areas or paved pathways through vegetables.

You should only use skips and trips to the dump as a last resort. Not only will recycling save you money, but it will also save our landfill sites from filling up with materials that others can use.

Personally, I like to undertake clearance work in one concentrated effort as opposed to tackling a bit here and there at different times. Obviously it's a matter for personal choice and your own particular timescale, but if you can do it in one go, the advantages are that you get everything out of the way and you're ready to continue your project unhampered.

WHY YOU SHOULDN'T DISPOSE OF OLD TURFS

If you're planning to scuff off turf to make way for a new lawn, patio area, pavement area, etc., you're going to need to give thought as to how to dispose of the old turfs. Before deciding to dispose of any turfs you might scuff off, let me tell you that old turfs will, given time, turn into the most beautiful, loamy compost that you can get. All you have to do to achieve excellent results is find an area in your garden where you can stack the turfs. Stack them upside down, so that the grass side is face downwards. Cover them with a tarpaulin and leave them for a couple of months or so. Then turn them over and you'll find the most wonderful soil for your borders.

OVERCOMING PROBLEM SITES

As I said earlier, it's unlikely that you'll ever have the perfect plot in terms of soil, aspect and climate. The important thing is that you're prepared to work with the site, and wherever possible overcome its problems.

Steep slopes

As well as problems with soil, aspect and climate, you may also find you have structural problems. For example, your garden may be on a particularly steep slope or on different levels. There are a number of ways you can make your garden more interesting and improve its general condition. However, don't be tempted to level off any slopes until you're sure there will be no structural comeback.

For example, I recently visited a number of gardens in Cornwall. Common to all the plots were the impossibly steep slopes, particularly in the front gardens where the height in relation to the public footpath below was frightening. When discussing the problems with the gardens' owners, they didn't see that there was any problem. Rather than attempt the impossible by levelling out their sites, they worked with what they had and layered their gardens in interesting and attractive ways. As one of them told me, the problem with trying to do anything else was that you'd risk interfering with a structure that was hundreds of years old and by doing so would risk all sorts of potential disasters.

If your plot has levels that you're unhappy with and you want as part of your new design to level out or significantly alter it in any way, you will need to employ a specialist surveyor to undertake a complete structural survey of your garden and advise you accordingly. Even were you to employ a professional landscaper or garden designer, they would need to have a survey report before working on possible new designs.

Your garden is basically a structured site. Whether it be flat, curved, sloping, steep or cut into a cliff face, there is a reason why the site is the way it is. So before you make any significant alterations to your levels, make sure that you're not going to bring your house down. Or worse, those of your neighbours!

Likewise, if you're planning to construct a new patio area where the ground is particularly steep, you should take expert advice as to what sort of base you will need to construct. Again, don't be afraid to discuss your plans with your local builder's merchant. Not only will they be able to help and advise you, but if you're in need of a good builder to help you with certain aspects of your project, it's here you'll find them.

Underground piping, wiring, cabling and sewerage

Not only do you have to be aware of the ground below your feet, but also what's beneath that ground in terms of underground cabling, wiring, sewerage networks, etc. If your house is a recently constructed property then you should be able to find details of the piping network or at least where the main piping system is from your conveyance documents. If you can't find anything among the paperwork you could contact the property developer and ask them for the site plans. Obviously it's important prior to digging down to excavate foundations for a patio or garden pond not to dig into the mains water system. If you do, and it's in your garden, you'll most likely have to stump up the costs of replacement or repair.

If your house is old and you have recently moved in, it's a good idea to speak first to any neighbours as to where everything underground might be. Although our garden is a tiny courtyard, beneath it is a series of sewerage and waste-water pipes, which not only feed from our property but also three of our neighbours. When we first moved in I wanted to remove the old slabs and would normally use a jackhammer to do this. However, because our house is part of an Edwardian terrace, it made sense that somewhere underneath our courtyard would be a sewerage system of sorts and we were right. So rather than use a jackhammer or anything that would shake the ground, potentially damaging the underground systems, we went down on hands and knees and chiselled each tile up. It was time-consuming and tedious and it set our work back a couple of weekends, but our sewerage system remained undamaged.

Whatever your site and its difficulties, take care when working on it. There's a whole underground system beneath most of our gardens that needs to be considered and protected. The last thing you want to do is to start your project and end up with a burst pipe in your first hour of working.

SKIP HIRE AND RUBBISH CLEARANCE

If you have to hire a builder's skip, you should be aware that they come in a variety of sizes, the most common being 2 yards, 4 yards and 6 yards. I generally go for a 6 yard skip and take the opportunity to get rid of all sorts of unwanted materials as well as debris from gardens.

If you cannot leave the skip on your own property and have to leave it on the road, you will need planning permission. Usually this will be arranged by the skip hire company who will charge you an additional fee for this, which will include mandatory planning application fees together with their administration charge. In my experience it's not very much, so if your skip hire company is asking for a relatively large amount make sure you query it or better still shop around. While planning permissions don't usually take very long to arrange, you should nevertheless arrange your skip as far in advance as you can. Few companies will be able to deliver a skip where planning permission is required without at least a fortnights' notice.

The other thing you need to allow for is the time to collect your skip when it is full. While most skip companies are usually quite prompt, you still need to allow them time for collection. Logistically running a skip hire business is difficult, as you have to plan to collect, deliver and unload all in one day. Builders and landscapers who regularly use skip hire companies are familiar with how it works, and don't expect the skip to be collected on the day they phone up. Anything from a day to a week is possible when it comes to collection. Remember also that bank holidays are particularly busy for skip hire companies as DIYers work on their latest projects. When it comes to skips, plan ahead.

WORKS REQUIRING PLANNING PERMISSION

Generally speaking, temporary wooden structures such as garden sheds and gazebos do not require planning permission. However, do check first with your Local Authority.

However, there are height restrictions on fencing. I've also worked on some gardens where the local authority has stipulated that the boundary fence can be no higher than 4ft tall and must be taken down to allow local authority access. While these conditions are somewhat unusual, and only came about as the property overlooked a river alongside which was a public right of way, it's nevertheless worthwhile contacting your local authority and finding out whether or not your proposed new structures require planning permission. Every area is different and it's impossible to give you blanket guidelines. So always check with your local authority that what you are proposing doesn't require planning consent or isn't in contravention of a conservation order.

FELLING TREES AND PLANNING CONSENTS

Even if they're on your own land, you'll need to be particularly careful that your local authority hasn't got either a tree preservation order or some other order that prohibits you from felling trees. It's quite common for there to be in place a number of restrictions and you really should check with your local authority's parks and landscapes department. If there is a tree order in place, it doesn't necessarily mean that you cannot ever cut the tree down, it simply means you need permission to do so. Which is why hiring a professional and suitably qualified tree surgeon is advisable. They will be able to make all the applications on your behalf, dealing with all the paperwork and permissions. Given their experience and relationship with the local authority, they'll usually be able to achieve this far quicker than you could working on your own.

Don't be tempted to avoid the issue of planning consents. In my experience those that do this generally end up creating more hassle and wasting more time that if they'd gone the legitimate route and checked things out first before starting work. Nothing will get the neighbours out quicker than the roar of a chain saw announcing the imminent death of a much-loved tree. If you go about things in the right way you'll save yourself stress and all the potential neighbourhood disputes.

◆ CHECKLIST ◆

- Decide as early as you can whether or not you're going to need specialist help with your project as you are likely to have to wait some time before contractors can begin the work.

- Choose your contractor carefully. Remember good gardeners are busy gardeners, so don't be put off by having to wait for them to fit you in.

- Don't be afraid to ask to see examples of contractor's work and if necessary speak to their customers. A professional company will have no objection to you doing this and most will even suggest it.

- Make sure you wear the right clothes and safety equipment when working in your garden.

- Either hire or buy the right tools.

- Make sure that whatever you're proposing doesn't fall foul of planning legislation.

- Generally speaking, felling trees requires the permission of your Local Authority.

- Never use a chainsaw unless you have undertaken the right training. It is far better to employ a qualified tree surgeon to undertake any tree-felling work. They can also apply to your Local Authority on your behalf for planning permission.

11

WORKING WITH SOFT FEATURES

TRANSPLANTING SHRUBS AND PLANTS

Whenever a client comes to me and tells me they'd like to have their garden made over, I first ask them how much they have available to spend. This question often has the effect on my client of raising a barrier and viewing me with some suspicion, as I suspect they think I'm about to drain their life savings or make them remortgage their home. However, once I explain that the reason I need to know is so that I can get an idea of what sort of makeover can be achieved they relax a little. Then when I explain to them that some of the most astonishing and dramatic gardening makeover effects can be achieved on virtually a shoestring budget, they are delighted. 'So what have you got in mind?' they usually say. 'Bearing in mind I'm on a limited budget.'

The first thing I do is walk with them round their garden. 'See that hydrangea over there?' I say. They nod. 'Do you know why it looks as if it's spent the last ten years growing on the side of the M25?' They shrug their shoulders. 'Because it's planted in the wrong place.'

As I explained previously, one of the reasons why plants and shrubs fail to survive and thrive is that they're usually in the wrong place, where their needs in terms of light, food and water are not properly catered for. It doesn't matter where you think they should go so they can show off those brilliant colours and marvellous foliage. If they're in the wrong place, they're not going to do very well.

So for the budget-conscious garden makeover, all that's often required is to redesign an existing planting scheme and move plants and shrubs to areas where they are more suited. Do this and almost instantaneously your garden is going to improve.

For those whose budget stretches beyond moving plants and shrubs to different locations, there will undoubtedly be situations where you will need to move something in order to make way for another feature, soft or otherwise.

Transplanting can also be necessary where overcrowding has occurred in borders. In fact, whenever I create a new border area I always overplant to begin with to avoid leaving the border looking bare and unfinished. Then as soon as the plants and shrubs establish themselves, I'm back in there thinning everything out and where appropriate transplanting shrubs to other areas in the garden where they will do greater good.

GUIDELINES FOR TRANSPLANTING

Before going any further, it should be noted that there are a number of shrubs that will not under any circumstances take to being moved. One that springs to mind is magnolia. This beautiful spring-flowering tree neither takes kindly to pruning nor being moved. So it's important before moving anything to check first that it's okay to transplant it. Most small trees, shrubs and plants are absolutely fine, provided you take proper care. If a shrub is already suffering because it is in the wrong place, then you've no alternative but to move it to better surroundings.

As a general rule you can move *deciduous* shrubs. These are shrubs that lose their foliage in the autumn, which grows afresh anytime after they have shed their leaves. This could be anywhere between late autumn and early spring. Take care not to move them when they are coming into leaf, ready for a new season.

Evergreen shrubs do not lose their leaves at all but should be moved in the autumn. The advantage of moving them at this time is that the ground is still usually quite warm after the summer season.

If time is against you, you can move evergreens in spring. First lay a piece of old carpet over the soil where the shrub is going to be planted. The benefit of this is that it will warm up the soil. If you've had a warm winter with no frosts for a while, you shouldn't have too many problems with the soil being too cold. If you get it wrong, and shortly after you've transplanted your evergreens you notice they are shedding their leaves, then this could be either as a result of a lack of water or the frozen ground. Don't despair though, as most shrubs will recover, although it could take a full season. However, conifers that suffer browning may never recover their green foliage, so take particular care with them.

Smaller shrubs

When transplanting small- to medium-sized shrubs you will need the following equipment and materials:

◆ Spade.
◆ Half-moon edging tool.
◆ Large tarpaulin sheet.
◆ Possibly a crowbar.
◆ Quality compost or garden mulch.

If the shrub is surrounded by grass or the ground is exceptionally hard, you should use your half-moon edging tool to line the circumference of the area that you intend to cut out. The secret to successful transplanting is to take as wide an area as possible in order not to disturb the root system and root ball of the shrub.

Once you've marked your area out, use your spade to dig all round the shrub and then dig down. Go as deep as you can to avoid damaging the root ball. Then with whatever additional help is available, lift the shrub out of the hole and onto the sheet of tarpaulin. Provided the shrub is small enough, wrap the sheet of tarpaulin around the base and root ball and then lift it into a wheelbarrow and take it to its new home. Larger shrubs can be dragged along by pulling them on the tarpaulin.

Prior to digging out your shrub, you should have dug out the hole where the shrub is going. Make sure you dig out a larger hole than the size of the shrub's root ball that you're digging out. Prior to lowering the shrub into the hole, spread a generous layer of compost or mulch. Once the shrub is in the hole, add some of the soil from the area where the shrub was taken. Backfill the hole using a mixture of compost and soil and firm it in with your heel. Top the hole up until such time as the ground is completely firm. If the shrub is particularly top heavy, you may need to stake it to ensure that it doesn't get blown over. Check the shrub regularly over the next few weeks to ensure that the ground is still firm and the shrub surviving. Water as necessary.

Very large shrubs

Very large shrubs and small trees require a great deal of pre-planning prior to moving. The first thing you need to do is choose the new location making sure that there is sufficient room for it to fit. In the past, I've miscalculated the area required to take a mature shrub. It's an easy mistake to make and can be avoided by measuring the height and spread (width) of the shrub you're planning to move, then checking it will fit into the area you have chosen.

The next stage is to dig a trench approximately 2ft around the circumference of the shrub you're going to move. If you can, do this some months before you move the shrub. The benefit of this is that you allow the shrub's root to be more contained and compact by the time it comes to move it. If time isn't with you and you have to move it immediately, then you should follow the same procedure but ensure that all the roots are neatly cut prior to the main dig-out.

When it comes to moving large shrubs you'll find the use of a crowbar makes things much easier. As you dig out your root ball area, use the crowbar as an under-lever to prise it out from the ground. You'll also need to cut any anchoring tap root and then carefully remove the whole shrub together with the large root ball and surrounding soil completely intact. It's unlikely that you will be able to this on your own, so make sure you recruit enough help before starting.

When planting the shrub in its new home, follow the above instructions and don't forget to apply lots of quality compost or mulch to the new planting site prior to lowering the shrub in. And once it's in, don't forget to water the shrub regularly until it shows signs that it is comfortable in its new home.

WHAT TO LOOK FOR WHEN BUYING CONTAINER SHRUBS

Just because a shrub is for sale in a garden centre it doesn't mean it is healthy. While not wishing to suggest that all garden centres do not look after their planting stock, there are some garden centres and DIY stores you would be best advised to steer clear of.

When I first started in my gardening business, most garden centres were family-owned or otherwise independently run businesses. Much of the container and root stock was actually grown on site and in the main the quality of the stock was superb. In recent years all this changed as garden centres went the way of supermarkets. Seemingly overnight, all the garden centres were owned by a small number of big-name multi-retailers, with the obvious and instant advantage that prices for shrubs and plants came down rapidly. The knock-on effect on the remaining small independent nurseries and garden centres was that many were put out of business.

In gardening terms, quality is priceless. You cannot put a value on a lovingly grown and cared for planting stock. There really is no substitute for the advice that an experienced, qualified grower can give when it comes to what shrub or plant to choose for your garden. Therefore I always advise my clients and everyone attending my workshops to seek out smaller, independent nurseries. For it's here without the dazzle of multi-million pound advertising campaigns, sofas and gismos where you'll find the most healthy shrubs and plants. Where the plants, shrubs and root stock are looked after by enthusiastic, passionate and qualified staff who understand pruning regimes and see plant care as more than simply hosing down the entire stock (and often the customers) in one fell swoop. Here you'll find your questions answered by knowledgeable, professional staff as opposed to a sales assistant who in the morning looks after the soft furnishings and pet-care products and spends the afternoon on 'outdoor' stock.

You should carefully examine every shrub and plant before you commit to purchasing them. Here are the things to look for:

How does the plant actually look? Nice healthy green leaves or are they spotted with rust and eaten away by aphids? Lopsided or straight growing? Unbalanced foliage where there are lots of leaves at the front of the shrub and nothing at all at the rear?

How about the branches? Are they evenly spaced, allowing air to circulate around the canopy, or is there lots of overcrowding with branches crossing over and growing into one another?

Press your finger gently into the soil at the top of the pot. How does it feel? Dry as a bone, waterlogged or just nicely moist as it should?

Does the plant look as if it's been in the pot for months or does it look nice and fresh? Are there weeds and moss growing on the soil's surface? A sure sign that the plant has been on sale for a long time.

If possible have a look underneath the container. Are there lots of roots growing out of the drainage holes or swelling apparent in the bottom of the plastic pot? If there are, then this is an indication of a root-bound plant, which is best avoided if at all possible. If you must purchase one, make sure you cut off the excess roots before trying to prise it from its container. My view on root-bound shrubs is that they've been too long sitting and will need more work bringing them on.

All these visual inspections are important in their own right. If the shrub is one that supposedly has a fragrance, then smell it. You'd be surprised how many so-called fragrant plants on sale in garden centres don't seem to smell of anything at all.

So right from the start, get into the habit of inspecting everything you buy. Although you shouldn't do as some rude people do and pull and shove everything about. Remember that until you've purchased whatever it is you're looking at, it's still someone's else's property. Be gentle here. Just quietly carry out a visual inspection and go with your gut feeling.

A worthwhile investment is a small, pocket plant and shrub guide. Take this with you whenever you visit a garden centre. In my experience there's a real lack of comprehensive information available on today's plant labels. Rather than any decent after-purchase plantcare advice, you get blanket advice. It can be difficult to find information on how tall something will grow and how long it will take to get there. This is where the pocket guide comes into its own. Rather than rely on what the mass growers want you to know and believe, you can source your own independent information there and then to help you make your decision. I always carry my pocket guides around with me in the van or car and I find them invaluable.

HOW TO TRANSPORT SHRUBS AND PLANTS

Sunroofs are for letting sun and air in to your car, not for acting as additional natural roof space for transporting your tall shrubs home. I can never understand why so many people seem to think it's okay to drive their plants home sticking out of windows, sunroofs, etc. Shrubs and plants need to be transported carefully and are easily damaged. If you're buying a large quantity of shrubs and plants or they are particularly tall or heavy, you should get the garden centre to deliver them for you. Even if they charge you for delivery, it's worth it to ensure your garden stock arrives in perfect condition.

When transporting tall and particularly heavy shrubs that won't fit in my high-topped van, I use a trailer and then lay the shrub or plant on its side, tied securely in place. Whatever you do, don't leave a shrub standing up straight in a trailer to be buffeted by the wind.

PLANTING SHRUBS FROM CONTAINERS

Watering is essential prior to removing the shrub from the container. My favourite method is to stand the container in a large bucket of water and then leave it for a while so that the soil is completely moist and the shrub can be easily removed. You should never have to force a shrub from its container. If you find that even after watering it won't slip out, you could use scissors to cut through the pot and remove the shrub. Once out of the container, you should tease some of the outer and bottom roots with your finger so they're no longer in the shape of the container.

Dig the hole for the shrub at least twice its size, making sure that you apply lots of quality compost or well-rotted manure, and then lower your shrub into its new home. Depending on the shrub's particular care requirements, it may be necessary to stake it to ensure straight growth and protection from wind. If you're living in an exposed, rural area you may find that you need to protect the roots from rabbits and the like.

Finally, beware of overnight frost and icy conditions as these are entirely unsuitable for any type of planting. No matter how tempted you might be to get those shrubs from their containers and into the ground, if there's frost, ice or even heavy rainfall, which makes the ground extremely wet and muddy, then wait until conditions improve. Good gardening is all about patience, timing and working with the seasons.

DIGGING OVER AND PREPARING SITES

When is the best time for digging?

If you've decided to dig over an old border, then ideally you should begin your digging in the autumn. As you dig over the soil, add lots of well-rotted compost or manure, which you can then leave to the winter frosts, rain and wind to break down. When the spring arrives, the soil will be nice and friable and ready for a final work-over before taking any planting.

If you can't dig over in the autumn, spring is also a good time. I've dug over gardens during the winter, but this has come about because of the requirements of a particular job. Certainly, given the choice, I wouldn't advise winter digging unless it's particularly mild, as the frost and ice really do make the ground rock solid.

For some unknown reason, some people begin their digging during the summer when the ground is like concrete. If you can, avoid summer digging. The soil really is too hard and you'll find yourself with an uphill battle. The benefits of digging over in the autumn cannot be overstated.

USING MECHANICAL DIGGERS

If you're planning to dig over a particularly large garden area, you may be tempted to hire in a self-operated mini-digger to save on the spade work. My advice is that you don't do this. While mini-diggers are extremely useful for digging out all sorts of areas like driveways and wall foundations, they aren't really a suitable substitute for digging by hand. One of the problems with a mini-digger is that when it digs it slices through the ground, and can't break the soil up the way you can working with a spade. You'll also find that the weight of the mini-digger will cause the area in which you are working to become very compacted.

CREATING A NEW BORDER

If you're creating a new border or planting area which was previously laid to lawn, you must first scuff off the top turf using the method outlined in Chapter 12. While you could simply single dig the area and turn the turfs over grass down, the result is never as good as getting rid of the top coat of lawn and working with the soil below.

Prior to starting work on creating a new border area, you must first refer to your Planting Plan. If all you're planning to plant in this new area is a number of shrubs or small trees, there's no need for you to dig over the area at all. All you have to do in this instance is dig out the holes for plant-ing, apply generous amounts of well-rotted manure and then plant whatever it is you've decided to plant.

If the new border area is to be home to a herbaceous planting arrangement or to take a wide variety of plants and shrubs, you should at least single dig the area so that the soil gets a good work over. If you notice that the ground is extremely hard, you can improve the texture of the soil by dig-ging in lots of sharp sand. As the gritty sand works its way through the soil it will allow more moisture and air to filter through. The advantage of this is that the soil will start to breathe again and in doing so will dramatically improve its potential.

Autumn composting

Remember that shrubs and plants will sap a lot of the soil's nutrients and goodness. So even if you're not planning to do any digging over of your existing borders, you should apply a layer of well-rotted manure or com-post over them in the autumn. You could also mix in some sharp sand or grit with the compost and then leave the whole lot to work its way into the soil over the winter months. Again this will have a dramatic effect on improving soil conditions and promoting future healthy growth.

DEALING WITH SEVERE WEED GROWTH

You may find when you inspect your borders that the entire area is covered with weeds and you're tempted to dig the soil over and pull them out as you go. Unfortunately, not all weeds are the same. Weeds grow either as part of a simple tap root system, where they grow upright, so pulling them up is easy, or they grow on an underground root network. Ground elder is an example of the latter. When you dig ground elder out, you actually aggravate the root network and by doing so generate more vigorous growth. If you have a border covered in weeds, you could either chemically treat the area, or treat the weeds organically.

The organic method is to cover the border in the autumn with a layer of old carpeting or matting. Leave it over the winter and remove it when spring arrives. You should find that by then the lack of light and air has killed off most of the growth. Rather than dig over the soil, pull out all the loose weeds that come away easily and then hoe the remainder of them.

Hoeing is a great eco-friendly way of controlling weeds. It's also physically undemanding as all you're doing is simply scuffing the top of the soil. The weeds are killed off as by removing their heads you take away their ability to take in air and light. Although initially they might return, over time their strength will be weakened and eventually they will die off. The benefit to you and your soil is you remain chemical-free, with a healthier and ultimately happier garden environment that's safe for you and your family.

◆ CHECKLIST ◆

- Most plants and shrubs can be transplanted to other areas of your garden.

- Autumn and spring are the best times for undertaking transplanting work.

- When purchasing any plants and shrubs, always check them carefully to make sure they are weed-free and haven't been sitting too long in the container.

- Be careful when transporting large shrubs from the garden centre. If possible, try to get them delivered.

- Preparation is the key to good gardening. Allow yourself plenty of time to prepare the soil to take your new plants and shrubs.

- Severe weed infestations should be given special attention. Allow yourself time to deal with them organically if possible, rather than simply spraying them with chemicals.

12

EVERYTHING YOU NEED TO KNOW ABOUT LAWNS

While it is beyond the scope of this book to give you detailed instructions on how to plant and prune every plant and shrub, I can offer you a rough guide on how to work with the most common soft features.

You'll have gathered that I'm an enormous fan of green lawns. Not only do they add all-year-round colour and interest to a garden, but their green shades create a welcome cool during the hot summer months.

REJUVENATING OR RENOVATING AN EXISTING LAWN

If your current lawn is looking tired and grass-bare, you could rejuvenate it rather than going to the trouble and expense of laying a new lawn. Later I'll show you what's involved in preparing for and laying a new lawn, but first let me explain why rejuvenating an old lawn can ultimately be more successful.

I'm imagining that your current lawn is in quite a state, perhaps with lots of moss growing in one area while other areas seem to be okay or it has a high proportion of weeds versus grass. Whatever the problem you have, it's important to realise that even if you remove the existing top layer of lawn and lay a new lawn, eventually the same problems that blight your existing lawn will resurface in your new lawn. The reason for this is that you haven't tackled the root problems first. It's a bit like repainting a previously damp wall without tackling the dampness. Initially the paint job will look brilliant, but soon after it will chip and crack as dampness works its way through the walls and back into the paint.

WHY LAWNS DON'T GROW

All poor-performing lawns are affected by one or a combination of the following factors:

◆ Poor lawn-cutting regime.
◆ Poor drainage.
◆ Lack of an ongoing preventative maintenance programme.

Whenever I lay a new lawn I give my clients full aftercare instructions. Unlike a new carpet, a lawn is a living thing and accordingly has a number of basic needs, which it must have to grow and prosper. These include not just the obvious ones, feed and water, but also things like light and air. One of the main reasons why lawns fail to perform is not because of a lack of food or water, but by a lack of light and air brought about by the blades being cut too short.

Many otherwise sensible gardeners seem to believe that for a lawn to look great it must be cut as short as board, which isn't the case. The problem with cutting a lawn too short is that the blades of grass are so low that they grow slower than weeds. Fairly soon the lawn becomes infested with unwanted weeds, which in turn reseed every time you cut the lawn, with the result that the problem perpetuates. As the blades of grass are too short to retain moisture, they simply don't grow as they should. The ground becomes increasingly compacted and the soil is denied any air flowing through it, with the result that it adopts a texture similar to concrete in which nothing apart from weeds will grow.

So the first step to rejuvenating and restoring your lawn to full health is to stop cutting it. How long you wait until the next cut will depend on what state your current lawn is in. If it's in a fairly poor state and you're in the growing season (spring and summer), then leave it a couple of weeks at least until you see some new growth reappearing. What you want to see are the long blades of grass that have wheatsheaf-like seed casings attached to them. As soon as you see these, you know that the lawn is in a position to start self-seeding and thus aiding its own recovery.

Whatever you do at this stage, do not apply any instant grass fixes that come in cans. You don't want any killers on your grass nor any false colourings. What you're aiming for is a complete and natural recovery. Things in cans generally speaking aren't natural, and while they will give an instant and entirely pleasing effect, you still really need to get to the bottom of the problem using good old-fashioned and entirely reliable techniques.

HOW TO RECOVER A LAWN

The stages I use to recover an old lawn are as follows:

1. Scarify the lawn using either a rake or a specially designed machine.
2. Aerate the ground and apply a dressing of sharp sand.
3. Apply a top dressing of seed and compost.
4. Leave the lawn sufficient time to recover and regenerate.
5. Continue with a preventative maintenance programme, including scarification and aeration.

Raking or scarifying the lawn

The problem with poor drainage is that it denies the lawn the opportunity to grow to its full potential. During the winter months the lawn will be waterlogged as there is nowhere for the rainfall to go, and during the summer months the lawn will be like concrete, resulting in lots of moss and weed growth. The only way to remove the moss is to rake it off. You can either do this yourself with a rake or hire or buy a scarifier from your local hire centre. Don't be alarmed if after using the machine your lawn resembles an end-of-season rugby pitch. This is exactly what the process is for. You're raking off all the dead moss, weeds, etc. and allowing the ground to get some air.

Aerate the soil and apply a dressing of sharp sand

Lawns are amazing things. We play football on them, walk on them, sit on them, stick spikes in them, cover them over with inflatable swimming pools, garden furniture, etc. and then wonder why they don't always look their best. One of the greatest problems lawns face is that essentially they are used as an outdoor carpet, with the result that the grass is regularly trodden on, scuffed and otherwise damaged. However, lawns generally recover quite quickly and grass will grow back in time. The greatest problem isn't so much damage to the blades of grass, but more that the soil becomes compacted, air no longer circulates beneath the soil, and ultimately the lawn fails. Without air getting into the soil, nothing will grow.

For example, flower borders are regularly hoed or raked over to get rid of weeds, as are vegetable plots. As well as acting as an essential weed-preventative measure, hoeing also turns the soil and allows air to work its way through the soil. Therefore the only way with a lawn to ensure that sufficient air is circulating through it is to aerate it, which is essentially to spike it. If your lawn is small enough you can aerate it by simply sinking your garden fork into the lawn at regular intervals up and down and across the lawn. Most lawn areas will be too big for this so you can either hire or purchase a lawn aerator, which is basically a giant spiking wheel which when moved presses itself into the soil. The end result is that your lawn area becomes peppered with long, deep holes that allow air and water to filter down into the soil.

Adding a dressing of sharp sand or lawn sand

When you have completely raked all of the dead debris from your lawn and aerated it, you're ready to apply a dressing of either sharp sand or lawn sand. These sands are very fine and when applied will work their way down the holes, helping to break up the compacted soil. Rain will help the sand work its way into the soil to create a far healthier environment for your lawn to grow and prosper.

Note: *Sharp sand can be an extremely unpleasant skin irritant. You should always wear gloves when handling it and read the safety instructions on the bag.*

Top dressing of seed and composts

There are a number of pre-mixed top dressing applications that are available in most garden centres or online outlets. Most top dressing mixes comprise seeds, compost and lawn sand.

However, my favourite method is to buy a good-quality, loamy top soil and mix it with a hardwearing lawn seed (read the box and find the seed that's suitable for your conditions). I also add some sharp sand to the mixture, which I then liberally apply over the existing lawn area once all the above preparations have been completed. Water if necessary and you'll find in a short time that the seed will start to germinate and root into the existing lawn.

RIDDING YOUR LAWN OF PESTS

Moles

If you're fortunate enough to be surrounded by rolling countryside, you will at some stage find your lawn area under attack from moles. These small, blind animals tunnel underground and at various points in your lawn you will find large deposits of the most beautiful, fine soil. Unfortunately another side effect of moles is that their tunnel networks are close to the surface of your lawn, causing damage to its structure, including potholing and large soft areas.

There are a number of humane ways you can rid your lawn of moles and by far the easiest is to purchase a relatively inexpensive ultrasonic device that you simply turn on and spike into the ground. It then sends a signal into the ground that will deter the moles. Generally speaking these small units are successful.

Another method of ridding moles from your lawn is to use an organic method of mole control. This method works because of the mole's heightened sense of smell. As they are blind, they have developed an acute sense of smell, which serves to warn them of impending danger. Moles are particularly wary of dogs. Therefore, all you have to do to is gather up some dog hair. Ask a neighbour or a friend who has a dog to help you out if you don't own your own. Brush the dog's coat and put the hairs into a netted bag. Old onion bags are great for this. Brush away the topsoil from the top of the mole hole, force the bag containing the dog hairs as far down the hole as you possibly can, and then leave the smell to do the rest.

As with anything in gardening, ridding your garden of problem moles won't happen overnight and the treatments take time, effort and a bit of imagination. Whenever you can, it's worth employing humane tactics for ridding yourself of moles as opposed to using poisons or traps. I've had the misfortune in the past of having to work in gardens where the owners have employed 'specialist' pest control companies. There's nothing pleasant about seeing a tiny, defenceless animal cutting itself to shreds in one of those awful traps. Undoubtedly moles are a great threat to lawns, but they can be dealt with effectively and humanely.

Worms and wormcasts

Another nuisance when it comes to lawns is the damage caused by worms. You might find that there are little piles of soil everywhere, similar to mole hills, but not as big. These are caused by worms pushing the soil up and usually occur when the weather is warm and conditions are damp or humid.

The way to rid your lawn of wormcasts is to brush them away using a soft brush. I like to wait until they have dried out sufficiently so the soil can be easily spread over the rest of the grass without going lumpy.

While moles are potentially devastating to your lawn area, worms are not. Worms are great for gardens and whenever you come across them you should make sure they're covered up so the birds won't get to them. Whenever I uncover a worm, I always cover it up again, even digging it a little hole to give it a head start.

If you haven't an area to dig your worms back in, then you could put them in your compost heap. Worms have an enormously positive effect on compost production. Indeed, there are companies that will ship you live worms bred especially for working through compost.

LEAVES ON LAWNS

If fallen leaves are allowed to remain on a lawn during the autumn and winter, they will cause problems. They will stop light and air getting to the lawn, but more importantly hot gasses will build up under the leaves. These gasses kill the lawn below and potentially contaminate the soil. Therefore leaves must be raked off lawns as soon as possible.

RESTORATION-SEASONAL TIMETABLE

Ideally, when restoring or renovating an existing lawn you should try to work to a seasonal calendar. Whatever you do, do not scarify a lawn during a hot summer as all you'll do is make the problem worse. Scarifying should be done preferably during the autumn and if this isn't possible you should aim for spring.

Top dressings should wherever possible be applied either in the autumn or spring, and again avoid working on your lawn during the hot summer months. The only beneficial summer lawn treatment is for you to aerate the lawn using a spiking machine or fork and of course to leave the grass to grow sufficiently long so as to promote healthy growth. Remember the shorter the grass, the more prone the lawn is going to be to weeds and moss. You'll also need to water more as your short grass will be unable to absorb as much natural moisture (overnight dew, etc.) as longer grass.

Seasonal calendar

Autumn: Scarify, aerate and top dress.
Winter: Ensure that any fallen leaves or debris are removed from the lawn.
Spring: Scarify, aerate and top dress, but only if you've missed autumn treatments.
Summer: Aerate only.

As you can see, there's more to lawns than simply a weekly cut. Don't be put off, however. Once your lawn is restored back to life, it really is very easy to keep it that way. The important thing is to work within the seasonal calendar and thereby take advantage of nature working with you. Weather really does help, whether it's the winter frosts working with your sand to break down the compacted soil or the overnight dew being absorbed by the longer blades of grass. It all helps towards a brilliant green lawn.

LAYING A NEW LAWN

If you haven't already got a lawn or you believe your lawn is too far gone and you would like to lay a new lawn, then the following guide will help you achieve your objective.

A great lawn is the result of preparation and not simply choosing the most expensive turf.

Going back to our damp room painting example, if you're not going to undertake the preparation necessary to rid the wood of dampness before repainting, fairly soon you'll end up with the same problems as you started out with. It's much the same when it comes to laying a new lawn. If all you're going to do is run some new turf rolls over a hastily prepared site, then save your time and money and don't bother, because you will end up exactly where you started in a matter of weeks.

SITE PREPARATION

How much preparatory work is needed will depend on what's currently occupying the area for your new lawn. For example, if the area is currently laid to concrete or hard standing then obviously you've got a substantial amount of work to do before you can even consider laying a new lawn. On the basis that your proposed new lawn area is not requiring the excavation and removal of concrete or similar, what follows is the preparation method I use for laying a new lawn.

Deal with any weeds

If one of the reasons you're laying a new lawn is because of the presence of weeds in your old lawn, then you're going to have to treat the weeds. You can do this using a chemical treatment available from garden centres. Simply measure out a quantity into your watering can (use an old watering can and dispose of it afterwards), add water and apply the solution to the entire site.

If your site has a large amount of deep-rooted weeds, which are common in lawns, you really should go to the time and effort of digging them out. In my experience this is the only way of treating them once and for all. The problems with the spray weedkillers is that they don't always kill off the roots and before long the weeds are back again. Although digging out weeds might seem tedious and initially time-consuming, think of all the future hours of work you're saving yourself by not having to worry about the weeds.

If you have a really bad weed problem, the most efficient and effective way of treating it is to wait till autumn then cover the entire proposed lawn site with old carpets, lino or whatever you can find. Spread it all over the area, held down with some bricks, then leave it over the winter. When spring arrives the effect of depriving the area of light and air will be dead grass and weeds. You're then ready to remove the top coat. Further chemical treatments or other work apart from removing the top coat may be necessary.

Removal of any top coat

Now remove any existing lawn. If the area is relatively small, you could do this by hand using a method called 'scuffing'. Work your way along the lawn with a half-moon cutter and line out spade-width channels, then scuff off the top coat using your spade.

An alternative, and far easier, method is to hire a turf cutter. These are petrol-driven machines with a top blade mechanism that will remove in neat rolls the top turf. The advantage of using a cutting machine is that you're able to remove a thin layer of lawn as opposed to taking off lots of otherwise healthy and beneficial topsoil.

Whatever method you use, don't forget that the turf you remove will, given time, make excellent topsoil. All you have to do is find somewhere out of the way in your garden, leave the turf laid out grass side down (so it dies due to lack of light and air) and in a few months' time you'll have the most wonderful loamy soil.

3. Soil preparations

Contrary to what you might have been told, I don't believe there is any benefit in digging over or otherwise tilling the soil in preparation for your new lawn. The problem when you dig over a site is that you break up the soil into lumps, which you then have to beat down into more pliable soil particles. The end result is that you then have to re-compact the soil so that there are no air pockets present, which isn't as easy a job as you think. In the past when I've come across or had to work on garden sites where the ground has been dug over, I've always left the ground for at least a couple of months to settle down.

Spiking

If the soil is completely compacted and the area hasn't recently been aerated, then now is the time to start sticking your fork into the ground. If the area is large, use a mechanical aerator. What you're aiming for is lines of small deep holes to allow the air into the soil.

Sand application

On the basis that you haven't dug over your site, the next step is for you to apply lots of sharp sand to the area, then rake it into the ground. The trick here is to rake gently. Don't dig the rake into the ground. Just work it gently over the site and you'll find that the sand will start to mix in with the soil, creating a nice layer of topsoil.

Walk the site

Putting your weight on your heels, walk over every inch of your site. As your heels press into the soil, this will have the effect of ensuring there are no air pockets below ground that could in time lead to hollows or lumps forming. I like to heel-walk the site then rake over the soil, followed by more heel-walking.

Levelling the site

Once you're satisfied that the ground is compact again and doesn't contain any soft spots or apparent air pockets, you can work at levelling the site.

The easiest way to do this is to simply:

1. Rake the soil back and forward until it sits level.
2. Walk over the entire area using your heels, creating firm indentations as you go.
3. Using a rake, level over the site once again so that you have filled all the pockets created by your walking, then firm in with your heel until the ground is level and hard.

DECIDING ON WHAT GRADE OF TURF TO BUY

Turfs come in a variety of grades, although most garden centres will usually only offer what is called amenity turf unless you specifically request a higher grade. My advice is that unless you're looking to create a bowling green in your garden that you opt for a quality, durable, amenity turf from a recognised quality grower. This is where price comes into play!

You'll regularly see lots of advertisements for turf at give-away prices. Don't be tempted. Good grass costs money and if you opt for a cheaper supplier you'll notice the difference as soon as you unroll it with its weeds, tears and general unevenness. Once you've laid this type of lawn you're on the battle bus from day one trying to improve it. However, if you buy a quality, but value-for-money turf, your lawn is off to a great start and you'll have many years of luscious grass to look forward to.

So how do you know which grass is good and which is terrible? The only real way to do this is to visit a number of garden centres. Don't even bother with the DIY chains as their philosophy will always be to stack 'em high and sell 'em cheap. You want the best quality your money can buy. When visiting the garden centres, ask the sales staff which company supplies them with their turf. Don't be surprised if they tell you they don't know, but ask politely if they would find out. Jot the name of the company down and then ask them which day their turf gets delivered. Note this as well and then ask the price per square metre. They'll usually tell you the price per roll, but make sure you know what that equates to in metres, as not all growers cut their turfs to the same measurements.

Once you've visited your local garden centres and gathered your information, you're ready if you can to do some online research. Quality growers will have websites giving details of their turf and growing procedures. A number of them will also have online calculators to tell you what quantities you need.

From your research you may be able to decide which grower is the one for you. However, I always think it's best to have an opportunity to see the turf before deciding. Now all you have to do is pop along to the garden centres on the evening of the day that they told you they normally get their turf deliveries and ask to see them. Don't just look at the turfs, unroll one just a little and see what the grass actually looks like. A good-quality amenity turf will have a sound and solid soil base and neatly trimmed, green, moist grass. With a quality turf, the grower usually cuts the grass immediately prior to cutting the turf. Often you can actually see some fresh-cut grass clippings on the top of some of the turfs.

What you want to avoid at all costs are the turfs that look dried out and have really crumbly soil bases. When growers grow turf they do so on a bed of plastic netting. While usually you can see this somewhere on the soil side of the turf, it shouldn't look as if it's about to come away from the soil. Everything should have a nice, firm feel about it and it should all appear moist. Even if the weather is particularly hot, it shouldn't have a dried-out appearance. In my experience, most garden centres don't do anything with their turf other than leave it outside in the midday sun with a sign up saying how much it costs. Which is why you want to be able to collect your turf order as soon as possible after it arrives, then get it laid on the same day if at all possible.

Once you have visited the garden centres and seen for yourself what the quality is like, you're ready to place your order. Remember, come sun or rain your turf will arrive so you really do need to be ready to lay it, which means all your preparations should be completely finished before you even think of placing your order.

And don't under any circumstances be tempted to wake up one Saturday morning and decide that today's the day to lay the new lawn and then go off trying to find some turf. You may think this sounds daft, and obviously it is, but I've come across plenty of otherwise sane people who've adopted this method and only afterwards, when trying to lay something with all the characteristics of a cheap roll of brown paper, have discovered that it's easier to find poor turf than quality turf.

While not wishing to knock other growers. I have always used *Rolawn* when buying turf. They are certainly not the cheapest choice, but I believe they cannot be beaten on quality.

MEASURING FOR TURF

Although this would appear to be the simplest part of the lawn-laying process, in my experience this is the area where most novice gardeners come unstuck. There are two things that you must get right when ordering your turf:

1. Order the right quantity of turf.
2. Ensure that you're ready to lay your turf on the day it is delivered or you collect it.

Ordering the right quantity

When you order your turf it will come in pre-cut rolls, the size of which will vary from supplier to supplier. Obviously you won't be able to order the exact quantity you will require. You'll need to order more than you actually need. As a rule of thumb you should order an additional 3% to allow for any cutting you might have to do. For example, if your lawn isn't square or rectangular you'll need to order additional turf to cover all the curved areas. In addition to the 3% extra, I always allow for an extra two rolls of turf in case of spoilage.

When turf is cut from the fields early in the morning, the rolls are stacked on top of each other on wooden pallets. These pallets are then loaded onto lorries for onward transportation. Owing to the high costs of transportation, most growers are forced to load up as many turfs on a pallet as they possibly can, which results in the bottom layers of turfs being put under pressure during the journey. Always allow for an additional few rolls as a precautionary measure, as nothing is worse than being just one or two rolls short and having to wait another week for them to arrive.

Ensuring you can lay the turf on the day of delivery

I know of no company in the UK that delivers turf to garden centres on Saturday mornings. So if you're planning to lay your garden on a Saturday morning and accordingly collect your pre-ordered turf from your garden centre on a Saturday morning, the chances are that those turfs will have been delivered some time during the week.

My view is that where possible turf should be laid on the day it is delivered to the garden centre. Remember that the turf rolls you are buying are areas of live grassland that have been cut off a field by a mechanical cutter sometime early in the morning or the middle of the night. They are then usually transported by unrefrigerated curtain-sided trailers or vehicles that are prone to heating up like a tent during hot weather, resulting in the turfs sweating. So by the time they reach the garden centre they've almost had it.

The only way to ensure that you give your new lawn the best start is to lay it as soon as you can after the delivery to the garden centre. So when ordering your turf, ask the sales staff on what day and at what time they actually take delivery. I've spent hours sitting outside my supplier's warehouse waiting for the turf to be delivered. As soon as the transport company pull up, I load from their truck to my trailer and then it's all hands on deck to get the lawn laid. I've actually laid lawns by floodlight to ensure that they are as fresh as possible.

LAYING THE TURF

Hopefully you'll get dry weather on the day you're going to lay your lawn, but of course this cannot be guaranteed. If it is wet, then the best thing to do is simply get on with it using the method I describe below. Don't worry too much that your new lawn looks discoloured because of the rain. That's not a big problem. It's only cosmetic and I've never yet had a disaster when laying a new lawn in the wet.

The worst weather you could have is scorching sunshine and intolerable heat. This is not only extremely uncomfortable to work in, but also the ground will be very dry and it can be difficult for the turf to 'bond' with the soil. If you are working in hot conditions, make sure you regularly spray the turfs that are waiting to be laid as well as gently spraying the soil you're about to lay the turf on. Concentrate on gentle applications of misty water. If you're too heavy with the watering, you could create pockets and dips where the water hits the dry soil.

Equipment needed to lay a new lawn includes:

◆ Something to cut the turfs with, so you can get them to fit into the shapes you want. I use a combination of scissors and Stanley knife. If you use scissors, make sure they're a pair you won't have to use again, as scissors that cut turfs don't generally enjoy a long life thereafter.
◆ At least two long, relatively lightweight planks that you can use as running boards for navigating your way round the site.
◆ A rake for raking over the soil immediately prior to laying the turf.
◆ A tamper. A tamper is a square wooden tool with a long handle on it. When you lay the turf on the ground you should gently 'tamp' it to ensure it bonds. You could also use the back of the rake, but do be careful with your tamping as you don't want to tear any of the turfs.
◆ Sprinkler hose.

Depending on your site, you can either lay your turf rolls across the lawn or up and down in rows. If your site is on an incline lay the turf across the slope as opposed to up and down it. By doing this you can ensure it doesn't slip and will bond more easily with the ground.

I always start laying turf at the point furthest away from the main hard-standing area. That way I don't have to walk over recently laid turfs to collect more to lay. I lay a running board over the prepared soil and then use this or a series of boards to navigate over and back across the ground without actually walking on the soil. Immediately prior to laying the next row of turfs, I gently rake out the soil to ensure that it's still level and there's sufficient tilth to seat the turf on.

You're obviously going to have to stand on one row of turf when laying the new row. Again use your running boards to do this. Never stand on recently laid turfs as the indentation of your foot will be evident in the new lawn. Simply lay your board along the other turfs and gently creep along while laying the next layer. Tamp the new turfs down as you go and once you've finished a row begin laying the new row at the opposite end. By doing this your new lawn will get the most pleasing striped effect as well as bonding better.

When laying your turfs in rows, lay the first turf down then lay the next one past it, leaving a tiny bit overhanging which you can then press down so that the turfs butt each other perfectly. What you want to avoid wherever possible are any gaps appearing between the turfs. If gaps appear, it's best to re-lay the turfs so they fit perfectly.

When laying the next row of turfs, you need to make sure that each turf doesn't end in exactly the same position as the turfs in the neighbouring row. If they do, you'll end up with lots of squares of lawn with bonding problems. The way around this is to cut off around a third of the first turf so that when you lay it, it doesn't end at the same position as its neighbour.

Turf is extremely pliable, so cutting it shouldn't be a problem. If you're going to create a circular lawn area or other such curved shape then you could simply lay the entire area as a square or rectangle to begin with. Then mark out your circle using twine or a hose pipe and use a half-moon edging tool to cut out the shape.

DEALING WITH PROBLEMS

Ends of turfs lifting

If the weather is particularly dry and hot you could find that the ends of turfs start to lift similar to the way paper does. This happens because the turfs are drying out, and is an indication that you need to do some watering. When you've finished watering, tamp down any edges that remain curled. You'll find that some edges may lift up during the first few days immediately after laying. The trick here is to be vigilant and keep gently tamping down the edges. Don't be tempted to ram them down into the ground as a once and for all measure. Persistence and a gentle approach are all that are required.

Gaps appearing in the lawn

You may wake up the morning after you've laid your new lawn to find the whole area is a mass of gaps between the turfs. This isn't altogether uncommon, so don't despair. What has happened is that the turfs have dried out and shrunk. The remedy is to water them back to life. Remember the ground beneath the turfs will be completely dry, so if you overwater or flood the area you risk dislodging the turfs. Again, be gentle. Set your sprinkler to a constant fine mist and then ensure that it works its way evenly across the lawn. When the turfs have once again become hydrated, you'll notice the gaps close and soon disappear.

In the event that any gaps do remain after you've finished watering and allowed sufficient time for the turfs to absorb the water, fill them in with some topsoil and then tamp it all in.

Be careful when lifting turfs

When I give a quote to lay a new lawn clients often query the price, saying they feel the labour rate to be excessive. Obviously these are people who have never actually laid a lawn themselves and experienced just how heavy turfs are.

Don't be tempted to do as some 'landscape gardeners' do, which is to either drop or throw turfs on the ground and then literally stamp them in. Although turfs are very pliable, they are also easily torn. Throwing them around, chucking them down or stamping them into the ground will ultimately lead to a poor-performing, problematic lawn.

The reason that so many people throw their turfs on the ground is that they're heavy, and having constantly to bend, lift and stoop is extremely hard work.

When lifting and placing turfs, always remember to bend your knees. If you're working on a larger area it really is backbreaking work, so allow yourself plenty of time to do the job, take regular breaks and use a wheel-barrow wherever possible to carry the turfs around. I run my wheelbarrow over the running boards to wherever I want to go so as to save as much lifting as possible.

When laying turfs you'll also find that you have to make a few adjustments as to their positioning, which again means more lifting and stretching. So don't forget to pre-arrange as much help as you can, paid or otherwise, and if you have any back problems you should consider employing a professional gardener to lay the turfs for you.

You should also always wear gardening gloves when handling turfs, as they can be quite an irritant on your skin. You'll also find that it's virtually impossible to wash off all the soil debris that will stick to your fingers and hands throughout the course of the job.

AFTERCARE FOR YOUR NEW LAWN

The days immediately after you've laid the turfs are crucial to your lawn's future success. You should ensure that your new lawn has sufficient water and doesn't dry out too much, without overwatering. Be on the lookout for any turfs that might die. Occasionally this can happen, particularly in extremely hot weather. If a turf does die, remove it from the area as soon as you can and replace it. Don't be tempted to leave it there in the hope of recovery. When turf fails, it does so quite spectacularly, first going yellow and then deteriorating further.

GROWING A NEW LAWN FROM SEED

Undoubtedly, garden purists will disagree with me when I say that I'm not a fan of growing a lawn from seed. While I cannot disagree that ultimately a lawn grown from seed will be a better lawn than one created using pre-grown, cut turf, I believe that the disadvantages of growing your own lawn far outweigh the advantages of buying in what is in fact a ready-made lawn.

The problem with growing a lawn from seed is that it is incredibly labour intensive. It also takes a lot longer for the lawn to establish itself, at least two or even three years. During the growing period you're faced with a variety of problems from birds pecking at your seeds to wind and rain either blowing or washing the seeds away. Even the most carefully prepared seeded lawn will have its problems when it comes to evenness. I've never yet sown a lawn from seed and witnessed a full and even growth right across the lawn area. Usually there are areas where the seed either doesn't germinate at all, or does so much later than the rest of the lawn. On top of all this you're going to have endless watering to do, which can be a real problem now that so many water companies have introduced hose-pipe and sprinkler bans.

My advice is that if you have lots of time on your hands and you're not too fussed when your garden is finished, then opt for the seed lawn. But if you want your garden to be finished this season and the lawn is going to be one of the main soft features, then turf is your best option.

Preparations for a seeded lawn are pretty much the same as for turf, although you'll need to consider if putting up netting to stop birds and the like from eating the seed is appropriate.

When raking over the soil you should be especially careful not to remove all the stones from your site. This is also true of turf preparations. By removing too many stones you affect the site's drainage potential. Few stones in the ground means that when the weather is hot, the soil becomes compacted. Then when and if the rains do fall, the water runs off the site as opposed to working its way down through the soil and giving much-needed benefit. By leaving the stones in the ground, they will create a structure which will allow the rain to filter through the soil. The grass will grow greener and taller as a result, which ultimately means fewer weeds.

The advantages of choosing seed over turf are that it's substantially cheaper, and that there are so many seed varieties to choose from. For example, you can choose seed mixtures for damp areas, shady areas, for playing football on or for using as a putting green for golf practice.

Ultimately it's up to you whether you choose seed or turf, but I hope that with the information I've given you you're at least in a better position to make up your mind about which is the most suitable for your needs.

◆ CHECKLIST ◆

◆ You'll have to decide whether it's worth rejuvenating or restoring your existing lawn, or laying a new one.

◆ Poor lawn performance is usually a result of either cutting the grass too short, or having no ongoing maintenance programme.

◆ When laying a new lawn, remember it's not just the new turfs that will create a good lawn, but also the preparation prior to laying them.

◆ There are lots of grades of turf available ranging from the terrible to the brilliant. Choose your turf carefully and don't base your decision simply on price.

◆ Once established, lawns don't need lots of watering. If your lawn goes brown, don't worry – it will recover once the hot weather is over.

◆ Planting a lawn from seed takes a lot more time and effort than using turfs.

13

FRUIT TREES AND HEDGES

PLANTING FRUIT TREES

Depending on the style of garden you are aiming for, you may wish to plant some fruit trees. Certainly fruit trees can enhance even the bleakest of garden plots and not only will they add much-needed colour and contrast, but they will also provide the household with fruit. Nothing beats the fun and satisfaction of growing and picking your own fruit. Over the years I've seen even the most determinedly disinterested of my clients become completely engrossed in gardening once their fruit trees have started worthwhile production.

CHOOSING FRUIT TREES

There are a whole variety of fruit trees to choose from, including apple, pear, plum and so on. Within each fruit there are lots of different varieties to choose from. For example, at the most basic level you can have eating apple trees or trees for producing cooking apple stock. My advice when choosing which variety of tree is suitable for your garden is to be guided by your own personal preferences in terms of the type of fruit you like to eat. Then visit your local nursery and discuss your preferences with the nursery staff. Be very careful about buying fruit trees from DIY chains and multi-retailers. When it comes to growing fruit in your garden, much of your future success will depend on the quality of the stock that you initially purchase. In my experience the only places where you can be guaranteed to get quality trees capable of producing fruit are specialist independent growers and nurseries. So it's worthwhile seeking out a good local nursery or arboretum and discussing your requirements with them.

STANDARDS, GOBLETS, ESPALIERS OR MS?

The terms Standard, Goblet and Espalier refer to the shape of a fruit tree.

When it comes to planting fruit trees, lots of novice gardeners are put off when they start to hear the nursery staff talk of espaliers and goblets and so on. So let me first explain the jargon and what sort of information you need to have with you so you won't feel either intimidated or lost when speaking to the nursery staff.

Standard trees

Ideal if you have lots of space available.

Fruit trees need plenty of sunshine and to have lots of air circulating around their branches. Therefore the space you allow for them is crucial to their fruit-production success. If they're too cramped they won't be able to get enough light and air, and consequently this will impact on their production capability.

If you've lots of open space the standard tree is ideal for you. The standard tree will need a space of approximately 4 to 5 metres (13 to 16ft) to grow. Bear in mind that depending on the type of tree you go for, you may well need two trees of the same species, but of a different variety, standing beside each other to allow them to cross-pollinate. The only way you can really find out which varieties will require two trees is to ask the nursery staff. This is where you need to be sure you're talking to experienced, qualified nurserymen as opposed to sales assistants.

When purchasing a standard fruit tree you should ask the nursery staff about the strength of the root-stocks. You'll also need to give them an idea of the type of soil that you are intending to plant your trees in. For example, is your soil clay, sand or chalk?

The stronger the root-stock, the larger your tree will ultimately be. However, the down side is that you will wait longer for your trees to produce fruit. Conversely, the weaker the root-stock, the quicker you can enjoy fruit production, but the disadvantage is that it will be for a shorter number of years than with stronger root-stock.

Generally speaking, standard trees will have strong root-stock and pre-trained trees, espalier and goblets, will have weaker root-stocks.

Espaliers and goblets
Ideal for when space is limited.

The reason espaliers and goblets are popular is that because of the way they are trained to grow, they take up less space than standard trees. Espaliers are ideal for planting against garden walls, where they will take up little space and fruit cropping is made relatively easy because of their location and size.

Lots of nurseries now sell fruit trees that have already been trained into espalier shapes. You'll see them on sale with wooden frames behind them. All you have to do is take them home, dig them in and either attach their existing framework to your walls or remove it and attach the already formed branches to your walls.

The advantage of having goblets is that they not only take up less room, but that their shape encourages and promotes excellent fruit growth. Neither is it necessary for you to buy young trees to prune into goblet shapes. You can work with existing trees or older root stock.

Don't be put off by limited space. Courtyard gardens are ideal places for espaliers, and these really do add interest and colour, with the added benefit of your own fruit production.

The Ms

When you hear nursery staff talking about the Ms, what they're referring to is the root-stock. For example, MM111 and M2 refer to vigorous root-stock that will ultimately produce large trees, while M27 refers to smaller stock, which would be ideal for use in trained forms such as espaliers.

My advice when you go to the nursery is not to try to sound knowledgeable, but ask for plain-language advice. As soon as you hear the Ms coming into the discussion, ask what they mean. Remember that nursery staff and growers will be used to talking in Ms and they are not trying to belittle or intimidate you. It's just the language they use.

WHEN TO PLANT FRUIT TREES

The planting time for fruit trees is ideally during the dormant season between autumn and spring. To plant a tree, dig its hole a few days before you actually want to plant it. Even if the soil is good, you should add some general-purpose fertiliser or whatever is recommended by the nurseryman. Where the soil is poor, make sure that you add a good bottom layer of well-rotted manure to the subsoil. Don't simply add cheap compost available from garden centres, but some really good, agricultural manure. Most independent nurseries will be able to provide you with the names of local farmers or businesses who can deliver it to your door.

When planting trees, make sure they are straight and firm in the soil. Depending on your site conditions, you should also consider providing wooden stakes for your trees. Again these will be available at the nursery, together with suitable rubber tree ties. Don't be put off by the cost of purchasing these tree ties. They have been specially designed not to damage trees by being super soft, yet super strong. I've seen many instances where gardeners have purchased quality tree stock and then skimped on the ties and used pieces of old rope or garden hose for securing the tree to the stake, with the result that the tie has quickly eaten into the tree. Don't be tempted to skimp at this late stage. Get some quality ties for your trees and then you're off to a really good start.

Personally I love fruit trees, and whenever I discuss a garden project with clients I always ask them to consider the benefits of including them in the new design.

A ROUGH GUIDE TO FRUIT TREE REQUIREMENTS

Apple
Apple and crab apple trees don't do well in sandy or excessively dry or chalky soil. If your soil is excessively dry or sandy you can build it up by adding in a mixture of quality topsoil and manure with the existing soil.

However, my own experience has been that it's more important to adopt the correct pruning regime when it comes to growing apples successfully rather than worrying about the soil. Although pruning fruit trees is specialised, there's no reason why you cannot learn it. Either buy or borrow a fruit tree pruning book or go on a fruit tree pruning course. Local horticultural colleges offer courses, so it's worthwhile checking to see what's available.

Cherry
Cherry trees will grow well in almost every type of soil except for water-logged conditions. When planting you should allow at least 5 metres (approx 16ft) between trees. Beware of gummosis, which affects diseased or damaged trees where the soil is too damp.

Peach
To be successful with peach trees, your soil will need to be well-drained and fertile, and not too chalky or acidic. Special care is needed when pruning peach trees as only the branches that have grown the previous year will actually bear fruit. Once they have fruited they will never bear fruit again. After harvesting the fruit you should cut back the fruit-bearing branches to allow the new shoots at the bottom to grow. In spring check on the new shoots and thin them out so you only leave four or so fruits on each branch.

Plum

Plum trees will thrive almost anywhere and make an excellent choice for any garden. There are no special growing requirements. However, plum does not fare well in exceptionally dry conditions, so if your soil is sandy, you should look to enhance it using the method described previously. When the tree is young you should ensure that it is trained into the desired shape as is it prone to cutting damage if this is done later. I had a client who had a plum tree, which she would never allow anyone near to cut. Eventually the tree got so out of shape that cutting was a necessity. However, as it was now a mature tree, it didn't take well to it and the tree never really recovered.

Fruit bushes – redcurrant, gooseberry and blackcurrant

You can plant your fruit bushes in any type of soil. Unlike the majority of fruit trees, currant bushes favour sandy soils, although this is not a requirement. You can plant fruit bushes from autumn to spring. Blackcurrants will fruit on the previous summer's wood so you must be careful when pruning. Ideally you should aim to prune in early autumn or if you cannot manage this then early spring at the latest. Remove up to a third of the oldest wood.

Unlike currants, gooseberries are pruned early to mid-summer when you should cut back all new side shoots to about five leaves. A second pruning is then required in winter to prune these back further to around two or three buds and half the length of the leading shoots.

Raspberry

Raspberry will do well in any soil. You'll need wire frames along which you can train the stalks to grow. Summer-fruiting varieties will bear fruit the following year, after which you should cut the stalk completely and it will be replaced by a new one.

SHRUBS FOR CREATING HEDGES

When working on your new garden plan you need to consider your boundary and perimeter borders. Obviously much will depend on the location of your property. For example, if you live in a remote area, you won't have to worry too much about being overlooked by neighbouring properties or suffering incessant traffic noise. However, if you live in a built-up area or on a busy road, a living boundary is an excellent and natural way of blocking out unwanted views or reducing unwanted noise. So rather than go for fencing or expensive walls, you could include a hedge in your design.

Even if you don't want or need to include a hedge as part of your boundaries, hedging can still be very useful for protecting planting borders from the wind and also gives them it a formal appearance. For example, a low-growing, tightly clipped box hedge makes for an excellent formal hedge to enclose a herb garden and give it increased prominence in the garden.

An escallonia hedge makes an excellent natural barrier for coastal vegetable gardens. As escallonia is relatively salt-tolerant, it will survive the harsh coastal conditions, acting as a protective barrier and will provide all-year-round colour with the added benefit of producing beautiful pale pink flowers during the summer.

WHICH SHRUBS ARE SUITABLE FOR HEDGES?

All sorts of shrubs can be used to create hedges. There's no need for you to stick rigidly to any one type. For example, you could create a mixed planted hedge including fuchsia, holly, berberis and escallonia.

Flowering hedges
Suitable shrubs: fuchsia, escallonia, forsythia and rosemary.

If you want to create brilliant variety in your hedge then plant a mix of shrubs and just let the whole lot grow and see what happens. Initially you'll find that some shrubs will naturally grow quicker than others, but given time the others will catch up to create a wonderful, interesting hedge.

Thorny hedges
Suitable shrubs: pyracantha 'Watereri', berberis, hawthorn, holly (*Ilex*) and rose.

Thorny hedges are ideal for areas where you might have unwanted intruders. For example, a very distressed lady contacted me with the problem that the local schoolchildren were using her front garden as a short cut on their way home. When she confronted them they became abusive and the problems worsened. After visiting her garden to see the problem for myself, I saw that the children had over a period of time burrowed their way through part of an escallonia hedge. My suggestion was that the damaged part of the hedge be replaced with mature thorny planting. We agreed on planting a mixture of mature pyracantha, berberis and holly, which had the immediate and dramatic effect of stopping the problem.

If you are concerned about potential intruders or deterring unwanted visitors, then a suitably chosen thorny hedge makes for an ideal natural deterrent. Similarly, if you are concerned about the possibility of intruders gaining access to your home via a ground-floor window, you could plant some thorny shrubs and bushes around the window area. Once they're established, cut them into shape and keep their levels parallel with the window ledge so you don't lose any light. Instantly you have created a naturally spiky deterrent.

Evergreen hedges

Suitable shrubs: griselinia, yew, holly, escallonia and laurel.

Griselinia is my all-time favourite shrub for creating a beautiful, dense hedge, which is quick growing and can be easily clipped and maintained. I've used this shrub successfully in a variety of conditions and gardens. I've even included it in our own tiny courtyard garden to disguise the wooden fencing that borders our neighbour's garden. Its qualities include being extremely tolerant of poor soil, wind and coastal conditions, as well as looking superb.

Although laurel is a very popular choice for hedging, and deservedly so, you must be careful when cutting and shaping it. One of the problems with laurel is that if you cut the leaves, the remaining foliage is prone to burning, so you end up with a hedge that has lots of unsightly brown and burnt leaves. The only real way to cut and shape a laurel hedge is to use your secateurs to cut either the branches back or the stems.

Whatever you choose, do consider including a hedge in your new garden plans. Not only do they act as great natural barriers and dividers, but hedges also make great nesting homes for birds and wildlife, which will enhance your garden.

◆ **CHECKLIST** ◆

- ◆ Whether or not you want to grow your own fruit is something only you can decide, but it's certainly worth considering.

- ◆ Even if space is limited and all you have is a courtyard garden, you can still grow your own fruit by using an espalier-shaped fruit tree.

- ◆ Fruit tree pruning is quite specialised. However, you can easily learn the techniques by borrowing a suitable book from your library.

- ◆ Hedges make great 'natural boundaries' and are an ideal way to reduce noise, increase privacy and, depending on the hedge you choose, keep unwanted intruders out of your garden.

14

CONSTRUCTING PONDS AND SHINGLE AREAS

CREATING A GARDEN POND

There are two ways that you can create your garden pond.

- Using a ready-made, pre-formed pool liner.
- Using a fabric pond liner.

There are advantages and disadvantages to using either method. The obvious advantage of the ready-made moulded liner is that you don't have to worry about coming up with a suitable shape. And the liner will also come with various pre-made levels inside the pond that will be suitable for sitting plants on.

The disadvantages of ready-made, pre-formed ponds are that they are relatively expensive compared to choosing a liner and they can be much more difficult to install in the garden. With the rigid liner you will have to excavate a hole replicating all the liner's dimensions. From experience, I can tell you this isn't always as easy as the manufacturers claim it to be. If you get it wrong you will find that the water doesn't sit level in the pond and your mistake is glaringly obvious for all to see. That said, I know lots of homeowners who are delighted with their pre-formed ponds.

INSTALLING A PRE-FORMED POND

As with any pond, you will need to choose an appropriate place to situate it.

Once you've chosen your site, you then need to mark out the ground that you will be excavating. You will need to excavate the site so that your new pond fits it completely. Don't worry too much if you don't get this right the first time. There's a bit of trial and error involved here. But initially do try to be as accurate as you can with your first excavation. If you go too deep, you'll have difficulty refilling the hole to a solid enough structure to take the pond liner.

Dig carefully to begin with. It's better to make the hole bigger as you go on, as opposed to creating something that is too big and having to backfill it. The way I excavate when using a fixed shape is to turn the mould upside down and measure its height. Next I measure the width of the highest point, which will be the pond's deepest point. Then I start to excavate to a few inches less than the deepest point and dig out the rest of the shape. Usually all that's then required is for a final dig out to ensure it all fits snugly. You can also use sand underneath the various levels of the pond. Before backfilling the surrounding area, lay a plank over the length of the pond, on top of which you should lay your spirit level. Ensure the pond is level. Then do the same again, only this time laying the plank over the width of the pond. I cannot stress too much that it's not enough to check the levels by eye. You really do need to use your spirit level. Nothing is more frustrating and will waste more of your time than discovering that the pond is leaning once you've filled it with water. On more than one occasion I've been called out by potential customers to ask me to repair their 'leaking pond'. When I've asked them what makes them think that it's leaking, invariably they've said: 'You can tell just by looking at it. One side of the water is higher than the other.'

Once you're satisfied with your levels, ensure the structure is firmly in place. To do this, put your hand on one side of the pond. If it doesn't sink down or flip up, you're ready to fill it.

Take care when filling the pond for the first time. You should allow a small quantity of water to flow in first and again ensure the structure remains level. Only when you're satisfied that the structure is solidly in place and shows no signs of sinking or falling off to one side should you finally fill it to the top.

To finish it off, you can spread a layer of soil over the bottom of the liner to accommodate the growing of aquatic plants. Or you could do as I prefer, which is to get a few bags of aquatic shingle from the garden centre, or use some pea shingle (wash it first) and spread this on the bottom. Either material will have the effect of dulling down the rather plasticy appearance of the liner and will help with the growing of aquatic plants.

USING A FABRIC LINER

Once you've worked out the size of your pond, you'll have to decide on a shape. I use pegs to mark out a square or rectangular area where the new pond is going to be, then using a non-toxic line spray marker I start experimenting with shapes. Be as creative as you like here, but remember that whatever you come up with you're going to have to work the fabric liner to fit it. Therefore you don't want too many folds if you can avoid them.

When you've decided on a shape, you're ready to dig. The average depth in the centre of the pond should be around 1 metre, roughly 3ft, which is ideal for growing most aquatic plants. Depending on whether or not you're going to have fish, and if so, what type, you may of course need to dig deeper.

Rarely will a garden pond only have one depth so you should look to create a shelf around the entire pond on which you can grow your marginals. The depth of this should be no greater than 30cm, roughly 1ft.

My advice when buying your liner is that you first work out the size of your intended pond in terms of width, length and approximate depth, then take the measurements to your garden or aquatic centre and ask them to work out what size liner you will need. Better still, take a digital photo of the excavated or the sprayed-on outline of the proposed site, which will make it even easier to work out how much liner you need.

When choosing a liner, always go for quality. There's lots of cheap rubbish available on the internet that I wouldn't waste my time with. Reputable manufacturers will always give you a guarantee with their liners and prior to deciding which one to buy, ask to see a few. After feeling a few, you'll begin to see why some are cheap. If they feel thin and not very strong, avoid them. Ultimately you get what you pay for. Always buy from a shop where you can actually feel and see what it is you're buying.

Once you've completed your digging you'll need to add some form of protective layer to the bottom to prevent the liner from being pierced. Most aquatic centres will sell you an underlay if you require. However, you can save yourself the expense by laying a layer of sand, carpet, felt or anything that's soft and durable.

You're now ready to lay your liner in the pond. When doing so, be sure to allow an ample overhang around the edges. Don't worry about this appearing unsightly as you'll be covering it up later.

Before filling the pond you'll need to anchor down the overhanging liner so as to stop it all from slipping into the pond under the weight of the water. You can use bricks, but I use unopened bags of sand as they're less likely to rip the liner.

When filling the pond do so very slowly to allow the liner to work its way into the various grooves and depths of the structure. Don't leave it to fill itself and then return, as you really need to ensure that the liner overhang isn't pulled in by the water. Tedious, I know, but the time spent monitoring its progress could save you hours of work later rectifying any problems.

As with a rigid liner, when you've finished filling the pond you can lay some soil or shingle on the bottom and on the marginal area to promote growth. When planting marginals, simply plant them into the shallow water directly. Most other deep-water aquatic plants come in plastic buckets, which I tend to leave them in as it makes it easier later when it comes to thinning out the growth.

Try to avoid introducing fish into your pond for at least a few weeks to give the whole pond time to settle and the water a chance to become more natural.

WATER PUMPS AND FOUNTAINS

It's always good to have some way of keeping the water circulating and there are lots of pumps on the market that will do this for you. You'll need to ask for advice on how powerful a pump you need, as again this will depend on a number of factors, including the size and depth of your pond as well as what you've got growing or living in it. Solar options are also available and I always urge my clients to look at these first.

BLENDING THE POND WITH ITS SURROUNDINGS

Of some importance is that your pond fits in with the overall garden and doesn't appear contrived with bits of either fabric or ready-made moulded liner showing. If you're going to brick or put rocks around the pond, then the secret is to allow them to overhang the edge. This way they disguise the liner and also make the side walls of the pond less obvious. Over time as the bricks and stones start to weather, the side walls underneath which have been kept in the shade will become similarly disguised.

Planting around the pond is also important. So many garden ponds are created using a pre-moulded liner, which is then allowed to sit like a sunken bathtub in the middle of the garden and look about as inspiring and natural as a plastic bag. Don't be afraid to put lots of tall plants and shrubs around the pond so as to keep it from immediate view from certain angles. By doing this you can create an element of surprise.

DECIDING ON FISH FOR YOUR POND

If you're planning to have fish in your pond, you should first research the type of fish you intend to have and from there work out what size of pond you will need. You can either do this by visiting your local aquarium or searching online under 'constructing a pond for keeping fish' or similar key phrase words. The type of fish you would like in your pond will dictate the volume of water you will need to accommodate them successfully.

A potential disadvantage of having fish in your pond is that they fall prey to birds. Unfortunately this means you'll need to have some netting in place, which can spoil the overall appearance of the pond.

CREATING SHINGLE AREAS

There's nothing wrong with creating shingle areas in your garden provided that what you create looks natural and uncontrived. For example, as opposed to simply covering one particular area with the same size and colour shingle, why not introduce come clusters of larger boulders, around which you could grow some flowing grasses? By doing this you immediately break up the monotony and potential grave-like effect that is so common when only one-sized stone is used. Aim for as natural as possible an effect as you can. For example, your stone area can be greatly enhanced by arranging clusters of grasses together with some additional taller planting.

Site preparation

If you're planning to shingle over an area that is already laid to lawn, you really need to scuff off the top turf and where necessary level the site. In the past when I've suggested this to clients and those attending my work-shops, a number have raised objections on the basis of what's the point in doing this. After all, the shingle covering will kill off the grass. While it's certainly true that the grass will be killed off once it's covered with a membrane and shingle, the area itself will be prone to being 'spongy', a bit like leaving a rotting carpet underneath your new laminate or wooden flooring. So it's important to remove the top coat of lawn. You'll also find that the lawn area is generally higher in places than the surrounding pavements or hard features. Over time as the lawn has grown and been tended to, the effect is that it swells above the rest of the garden. Were you to cover this area with shingle without any preparations, you're going to find that the shingle area is higher than the lawn area, with the potential problem of having the shingle rolling down onto pathways or driveways.

The preparation method is as follows:

1. Remove the top layer of turf either by scuffing it off using a spade or if the area is large, by using a mechanical turf cutter.
2. Survey the site to ensure that it is deep enough to take the shingle and that the new stone area will not be higher than surrounding paths, driveways, etc.
3. If necessary, excavate further soil to create a deep enough area to accommodate the shingle.
4. Lay a proper weed-preventative membrane over the entire surface.
5. Mark out and create any planting areas.
6. Fill in the shingle, which will need to be washed off using a hose and then raked level.

WEED-PREVENTATIVE MEMBRANE

I've seen all sorts of money-saving weed-preventative membranes used, ranging from old carpets and lino to cutting up the plastic bags that the shingle came in and then using them as a groundsheet.

All of these methods are entirely useless. Lino and carpets will not allow the water to drain off the site, and thus you'll end up with areas of water-logging, while the plastic bags will quickly become brittle through weathering and will eventually crack and tear. Fairly soon your shingle area will be covered with weeds and unsightly pieces of plastic sticking up out of the ground.

Quality weed-preventative membranes, or 'landscaping fabric', are available in most garden and building centres. This fabric is especially designed to be breathable and to allow the water to seep through it. Therefore you won't have any problem with your site waterlogging and if you have created any planting areas they'll benefit from rainwater and dew.

If the area you're working is relatively large then you're probably better off visiting your local builder's merchant and buying a large roll of membrane, making sure to tell them that you want it for landscaping.

I've always found it useful to buy some mushroom pegs, which I use to peg down the corners prior to laying the shingle. Similar to when constructing a pond, you should always allow for plenty of overhanging membrane. Once you've finished laying the shingle and raked it over, allow it to settle for a day or more before cutting off the overhanging membrane so that none of it shows. My advice is to leave the mushroom pegs in as this will stop the membrane from shifting.

PLANTING IN SHINGLE

Provided you haven't already laid your shingle, all you have to do to plant in it is to put your plants into the ground prior to laying your membrane. When doing this, make sure you add lots of quality, rich compost as over time the soil's natural nutrients will be somewhat eroded by being covered up. I also dig large planting holes when planting anything in shingle and then lay a really good layer of compost mixed with topsoil and even a bit of sand or grit to help with drainage. Once you've completed your planting, lay your membrane fabric over the entire area including the planted areas and then cut out holes to allow the plants to poke out. The advantage of doing it this way is that you won't end up with lots of cuts and edges surrounding the plants, which will in time start to lift up and allow weeds through.

If you've already got your shingle laid and you want to create a planting area, then all you have to do is rake back an area of shingle of approximately three times the size of the planting area you wish to create. Using scissors or a Stanley knife, cut an X in the middle of the membrane fabric where you want the centre of the bed to be. Pull back the fabric in a star shape, which will have been created by cutting the X.

Once you've pulled the fabric back, you'll most likely find that the soil has a rubbery appearance and is completely compacted. What I do in this case is dig out the entire area to about a double spade's depth and lay it on a piece of tarpaulin. If possible I work over this soil with a mixture of compost, sand and topsoil to create a better loam. I then dig down the remainder of the hole to the required depth to take the plants or shrubs and lay a layer of quality compost. Then using the improved loamy soil I backfill around the plants and firm it with my heels.

I then lay the membrane back down and if necessary peg down some of the corners. The shingle is then raked back over again and the job is done.

If you are creating planting areas in existing shingle, do take the time to improve the soil. Remember that because the soil has been under the stones for so long it hasn't had a chance of having light or air get to it, thereby reducing its growing potential.

Don't forget to regularly feed planting in your shingle area in the first year's season. Obviously once the shrubbery has established itself, and shows healthy signs in term of overall size, leaf growth and so on, regular feeding may not be necessary, but initially you should do all you can to help the plants establish themselves.

When choosing plants for shingle areas you need to ensure that what you're putting in will take to a rocky environment. When looking for inspiration at what grows well in stony conditions, visit the coast. Here you'll find all sorts of grasses and varieties of sea cabbages thriving. Whatever you do, don't pick them from the beach as this is not only possibly illegal depending on the location, but you're also damaging a natural habitat and environment. It's far better to take some photographs of the planting arrangements, which you can then take home to study. Look at the way that natural clusters of grasses work in terms of layout and size, then visit your local garden centres and look for similar plants on sale.

CREATING PLANTING BEDS IN SHINGLE AREAS

There's no reason why you should limit your planting to limited clusters of plants underneath the shingle. A wonderful and inspirational alternative is to construct some planting beds. You can either go for raised beds, or simply build them into the scheme.

My favourite material for constructing beds in shingle areas is old railway sleepers, which you can arrange in a variety of shapes. Instead of shingling all the area, first construct your beds using the sleepers and then shingle in all around them. The advantage of this is that you're not then limited to plants that will only tolerate the relatively harsh and barren conditions created by the shingle. You can also use the sleepers to create raised beds so that they are easier to work on, which is particularly useful if you have mobility problems and don't want to spend your gardening time on your knees.

Old water barrels can also be half-sunk at angles to create alternative planting beds. In fact, you can use anything from unwanted bathtubs to sinks to create something different. The important thing is to have some form of natural planting to take away from the harshness of the stones. Whether you go for a minimalist scheme or bold, brash planting is up to you.

USING DECORATIVE BARK

Decorative bark is an ideal way of keeping down weeds in borders and also of helping the soil to retain moisture. The way it works is that you simply sprinkle it over the soil in your borders without using any weed-preventative membrane. Thus it won't hinder or interfere with any bulbs or herbaceous plants that may come up.

However, I often come across homeowners who see bark as the softer alternative to shingle or aggregate and lay it everywhere, instead of using it as a decorative mulch or soil enhancer, which is what it really is. They lay a membrane and cover it with bark. The result is disappointing to say the least. The problem with bark chippings is that they dry out easily, more especially when they are sitting on top of fabric liner as opposed to soil. As they dry out they become significantly lighter, which means they're easily blown around the rest of the garden and of course the birds love nothing better than picking through them and discarding the chippings where you least want them.

So if you are thinking of adding decorative bark chippings to your garden, then do so as part of a plan to improve soil conditions as opposed to a low-maintenance design.

If you have children and you're having bark in your garden, make sure that the bark you buy is non-toxic and child-friendly. Remember also that if you have very small children, bark is a real temptation for small hands and mouths to explore, so you need to weigh up whether or not it's a suitable material for your own personal circumstances.

◆ CHECKLIST ◆

- ◆ If you're having a pond in your new garden you need to decide on whether you're going to use a rigid, pre-formed liner or a fabric liner.

- ◆ Rigid liners are more difficult to install than fabric liners.

- ◆ If you're planning to have fish in your pond, you need to take expert advice on how big your pond should be, based on the type and quantity of fish you intend to keep.

- ◆ If you're having an area of your new garden laid to shingle, you must first lay a suitable weed-preventative membrane, which not only prevents weeds from growing up, but also allows water to soak away.

- ◆ Planting in your shingle area will greatly enhance its appearance and make it far more alive and interesting.

- ◆ Bark is an excellent mulch. However, you should be careful when using it if you have children.

- ◆ In hot weather, bark chippings dry out and become lighter, making them prone to being blown around your garden, which can look unsightly.

15

SEASONAL CALENDAR AND PLANTS FOR DIFFICULT PLACES

SEASONAL CHANGES AND GLOBAL WARMING

Undoubtedly the effects of global warming are impacting on the gardening calendar. A noticeable effect is that we seem to be having milder winters. Without the benefit of harsh frosts, pests and aphids are not being killed off as they previously were. The impact of this can been see in areas such as fruit production, with the unfortunate result that the following year's fruit crop isn't as good as it could have been as the pests have been able to continue with their damage.

Although this is just one small change, there are and will be others. However, when it comes to nature, we should never underestimate its ability to adapt.

I believe the most likely problem for us as gardeners will be the increasingly hot weather and the accompanying lack of water. Therefore it's important that you consider including at least some drought-resistant planting in your new garden. And of course, wherever possible you include as many natural sources of water as you can, for example, installing not one but numerous water butts and using 'grey' water for watering fruit and vegetables.

You should never worry about your lawn browning and burning. Obviously you'd do well to follow the maintenance regime for lawns outlined in Chapter 12, but remember that brown lawns quickly recover once the autumn arrives and the ground becomes moist. So don't waste precious water on lawns. One of my pet hates is to see sprinklers spraying lawns when the rest of us are doing all we can to reduce our water consumption.

Watering trees isn't necessary. As well as running a gardening business, I also have a lease on a local boating lake. The area is surrounded by trees, which include silver birch. Usually these trees don't lose their leaves until autumn. However, in 2006 they began shedding their leaves in July and by the time August had arrived they looked positively barren, which prompted visitors to our lake to ask why all the trees had died.

They hadn't actually died. What had happened was that because of the exceptionally hot weather, the trees had perceived a threat to their well-being and faced with a potential ongoing lack of water had decided to shed their leaves in an effort to save their need for water consumption.

While aesthetically we may be disappointed that the trees don't look as lush as they usually do, we should be in awe of natures ability to protect itself when faced with adversity. This is why there is no need to water trees, other than those that you have just recently planted. In fact, if you do water trees you run the risk of damaging them as they will become lazy. Most trees will absorb water through their leaves, but also through their roots. The more difficult it becomes for them to source water, the more they grow their roots in search of water, which in turn gives them a more solid foundation. However, if you regularly water them, you stop them from feeling it's necessary to grow their roots, with the result that you end up with a tree that has shallow roots, which makes it vulnerable to being blown over in strong winds.

When it comes to protecting your garden from climatic change, you should remember that nature is far more powerful and resourceful than we can ever be. Your garden will evolve and develop to adapt to its changing environment and therefore you should only intervene with those shrubs and plants that really do need water to survive, for example hydrangeas and vegetables.

GUIDE TO SEASONAL PLANTING

Winter

I've always enjoyed winter gardening. There's nothing better than getting out on a bright, sunny winter's day and working yourself warm. Despite the inhospitable conditions, there's quite a lot to be done in the garden. Tasks include:

◆ Continuing with the autumnal tidy-up.
◆ Rose pruning.
◆ Wisteria pruning.
◆ Repairing and replacing wooden features such as sheds and fencing.
◆ Staking everything that could be damaged during winter weather conditions.
◆ Wrapping up in fleece or straw blankets any tender tropical plants.
◆ Winter digging.
◆ Planting (see list below).

Generally speaking most planting will be undertaken in either spring or autumn. However, there are a number of things that can be planted during winter, including:

◆ Aromatic herbs.
◆ Bulbs for spring flowering (early winter).
◆ Roses.
◆ Bare rooted shrubs.
◆ Heathers.
◆ Hedges (depending on the shrubs you're using).
◆ Trees.

◆ Flowering shrubs.
◆ Rhododendrons.

Spring

Spring is the busiest season for gardeners. This is the time when everything starts to wake up after the winter dormant season.

This is the season for continuing work on restoring your lawn, or if you're planning a new one, now is the time to lay it.

Spring is an excellent time for planting. As the ground warms up after the cold winter, conditions become ideal. Some of the most common things to plant in spring include:

◆ Herbs, including parsley, fennel, dill, coriander, marjoram and thyme.
◆ Vegetables, including peas, potatoes, onion sets and lettuces.
◆ Conifers.
◆ Box.
◆ Bamboo.
◆ Clematis.
◆ Most biennials.
◆ Lawns.
◆ Most perennials.

Summer

This is the time of course to plant your summer bedding, create those magnificent hanging baskets and bring colour to every corner of your garden.

Usually, the hot weather in summer makes it less than ideal for planting and you really should aim to have your planting completed in the spring. Lawns are particularly prone to dying off in the hot weather and it is certainly not, despite what the garden centre advertisements say, the best time to lay a new lawn.

However, summer is an ideal time for you to plant your aquatic plants, as well as tropical bamboos. Irises and lilies can also be planted.

In the vegetable garden work will continue with harvesting crops and you can also sow lettuce, spinach, beetroot, spring cabbage and turnips.

Autumn

Autumn is the time of year when gardeners everywhere clear out, cut back and generally tidy up the season's growth. There is also an opportunity to plant a number of things including:

◆ Laying a new lawn.
◆ Clematis.
◆ Hedges.
◆ Biennials.
◆ Flowering shrubs.
◆ Rhododendrons.

PLANTING FOR DIFFICULT AREAS

Few if any of us will ever be lucky enough to have the perfect site for our gardens. Having worked in all sorts of different gardens with clients with equally different budgets, I can tell you that's it not money or aspect that creates the magnificent garden, but perseverance and enthusiasm and most importantly a willingness to adapt to the conditions. Wherever possible you should also look to improve your conditions. For example, if your soil is poor, you should work at improving it. Similarly, if there are areas in your garden where nothing seems to grow then you should investigate why.

In my experience, the most common reason for things not growing somewhere is that they've been planted in the wrong place. The right plant in the wrong place is going nowhere, so take a bit of time to do research prior to purchasing shrubs, plants or sowing seed.

Don't always be guided by what the sales staff tell you. Carry out your own research and don't be afraid to ask the garden centre staff as many questions as you need answers. When you start asking sales staff questions, it soon becomes apparent whether or not they actually know what they're talking about. In the past I've overhead garden centre staff give prospective customers the most appalling and inaccurate advice. So it really does pay to go to either a specialist nursery or one of the few remaining independent nurseries where the advice is given by knowledgeable, experienced staff, many of whom will have grown, planted or grafted whatever it is you're looking to purchase.

The following list of plants and shrubs for 'problem areas' is by no means definitive, but it gives you a starting point:

Damp shady areas

Hydrangeas, camellias, ferns, astilbe, hosta, polygonatum adoratum.

Dry shady areas

Cyclamen, *acuba japonica*, snowberry, *Daphne laureloa*, geranium, *Skimmia japonica*, viburnum.

Windy areas

Spiraea, *Salix*, laburnum, philadelphus (mock orange), hawthorn.

Areas with predominantly chalky soil

Scabious, tree poppy, oriental poppy, St John's wort, clematis.

THE BENEFIT OF A PLANT FINDER

My advice if you're new to plants and shrubs is to buy or borrow a good plant finder. Some clients at my workshops have purchased CD plant finder software, but I prefer one of the pocket-sized books, the main advantage being that you can always have it with you.

Most of these books will also include other essential information, such as what time of the year to plant, prune, cut back, divide, etc. as well as which position best suits the plant or shrub.

A FINAL WORD OF ENCOURAGEMENT

I hope that you have found the information, advice and exercises in this book helpful. As I said on the first page, gardening is great fun. I love gardening and over the years I've solved many a personal dilemma while pottering away among the plants and shrubs. I've seen the lives of the most reluctant gardeners turned around as they discover the magic that is gardening. What greater hope is there for a better world than to see someone undertaking planting in the autumn in anticipation that come the spring their labours will be rewarded with new growth? What greater pleasure is there than spending enjoyable time relaxing in the privacy and beauty of your own garden while all around you the world rushes by?

My final bit of advice to you is this. If at any time you feel the fun going out of your gardening, put the kettle on, brew your favourite beverage and remind yourself that gardening is nothing if it's not fun. Then return to whatever was making you unhappy or frustrated and look for a better way of doing it.

In the past when I've struggled with some aspect of my gardening, I've realised that nature always knows best. And to learn from the plants themselves as opposed to what it says or doesn't say on the labels.

A good gardener is someone who realises that they will never know it all. But a great gardener is someone who sees plants as the future, as the focal point, and everything else in the garden – the patios, arbours, swinging seats, walls and so on – as simply places from where we can sit and enjoy the beauty of our garden and the tranquillity and satisfaction that comes when we realise that we've done our bit to help it all along.

If you want to contact me to share your experiences, whether they be good, bad or otherwise, please visit my website at: www.PaulPower.co.uk

Best of luck!
Paul Power

INDEX